Electronic Highway

ROBBERY

D0218770

An **artist**'s guide

to **copyrights**

in the **digital** era

Mary E. Carter

Electronic Highway ROBBERY
An Artist's Guide to Copyrights in the Digital Era

Mary E. Carter

Peachpit Press
2414 Sixth Street
Berkeley, CA 94710
510/548-4393
800/283-9444
510/548-5991 FAX

Find us on the World Wide Web at:
http://www.peachpit.com

Peachpit Press is a division of Addison Wesley Longman
Copyright © 1996 by Mary E. Carter

Cover design: Mimi Heft and Gary W. Priester
Cover illustration: Gary W. Priester
Interior design: ProImage and Mimi Heft
Page Layout: ProImage
Editing: Karen Winters and Ted Nace
Legal Edit: Brad Bunnin
Editorial Management: Roslyn Bullas
Editorial Assistance: Kaethin Prizer
Copyediting: John Hammett
Indexing: Rebecca Plunkett

Permissions
The author gratefully acknowledges the following people and organizations for assistance in obtaining permission to use quoted materials and copies of artwork and photographs:

Agence Photographique de la Réunion des Musées Nationaux for *The Balcony* by Edouard Manet; Artists Rights Society; John Perry Barlow; Cameraphoto/Art Resource, NY for *L.H.O.O.Q.* by Marcel Duchamp; Esther Dyson, EDVenture Holdings, Inc.; FPG International and James Porto for *Clock Headed Business People in Desert*; Harper Collins Publishers and Anne Wells Branscomb; Herscovici/Art Resource, New York, for *Perspective II: Manet's Balcony* by Rene Magritte; Alfred A. Knopf, Inc.; Loompanics Unlimited and Dennis Fiery; Penguin USA; Stecher Jaglom & Prutzman and Art Rogers for *Puppies*; Bruce Sterling; Tony Stone Images and Nick Vedros for *Potawatamie Indian*; Joe Viesti/Viesti Associates for *Dallas Skyline*; and The WELL/Whole Earth 'Lectronic Link.

ISBN 0-201-88393-7

9 8 7 6 5 4 3 2 1

Printed and bound in the United States of America

(soy bean ink and union bugs as applicable)

In memory of my Grandma, **Jennie***,*
poet and linotype operator,
and my mother, **Mary***,*
teacher.

Acknowledgments

This book came about due to the generosity of many people. I want to thank each and every one of them for their time, their advice, their original thinking.

For bringing to my attention the need for such a book, I thank my agent, **Matt Wagner**. Always willing to talk, funny, and supportive. Thanks, Matt.

I thank my editor and long-time friend **Karen Winters**. She gave me structure and focus, and kept me from embarrassing myself too badly.

For cheerfully allowing me to play "stump the professor," thank you **Paul Pratchenko**, artist and teacher, raconteur of the fine arts, and good neighbor. Thank you **Margie Pratchenko** for giving me your actor's insights when I flagged.

Thank you **Barb Hauser**, my dear friend and rep, for your unflagging warm support, words of encouragement, and common sense.

Special thank yous to artist representatives **Jan Collier**, **Barbara Gordon**, **Corey Graham**, **Pat Hackett**, **Richard Salzman**, and **Ron Sweet**. Thanks, too, to the advertising agency art directors who were willing to talk about comping.

Thanks to all of the attorneys who contributed to my research: **Donald Buder** of Mandel Buder & Jacobsen in San Francisco; **Roberta Cairny** of Fenwick & West in San Francisco; **Terry Carroll** of Cooley Godward Castro Huddleston & Tatum in Palo Alto; **Tad Crawford**, Attorney at Law and contributing editor to *Communication Arts* magazine; **Adrienne Crew** at California Lawyers for the Arts; **Russell Jackman**, Attorney at Law in Sacramento; **Curtis Karnow** of Landels, Ripley & Diamond in San Francisco; **Lisa Kenkel**, Attorney at Law, Corel Corporation; **Jeffrey O'Connell** of Shartsis, Friese & Ginsburg in San Francisco; **Marc Paisin**, Attorney at Law in Oakland; **Valerie Patten**, Attorney at Law in Menlo Park; **Donald Prutzman** of Stecher Jaglom & Prutzman in New York; **Jeffrey Selman** of Severson & Werson in San Francisco; and **Karen Shorofsky** of Steinhart & Falconer in San Francisco.

Thank you for your time and insights and for allowing me to quote your work, **Esther Dyson**.

Thanks to **Alma Robinson** and everyone at **California Lawyers for the Arts** for answering my many questions and for guiding me to appropriate readings on copyright law.

Thanks to the editorial and design team that worked on the book: **Gary W. Priester** (cover design and illustration), **Mimi Heft** (cover and interior

v

design), **Jimmie Young** of **ProImage** (interior design and layout), **Karen Winters** (editing), **Ted Nace** (editing), **Brad Bunnin** (legal edit), **John Hammett** (copyediting), **Roslyn Bullas** (editorial management), **Kaethin Prizer** (editiorial assistance), and **Rebecca Plunkett** (indexing).

For online friends, a very special thank you for being there, answering my interminable questions, and freely giving me tips and leads: **Andre Bacard, Reva Basch, Gareth Branwyn, Hilarie Gardner, Michael L. Gaylord, Mike Godwin, David Hawkins, Clifford Pickover, Howard Rheingold, John Sledd, Lee Tien, Daniel Will-Harris,** and special thanks to **Bruce Sterling** who allowed me to quote from his online comments. Thanks for your input to my copyright topic posted on the **Electronic Frontier Foundation Conference** at The WELL: **Branzburg V. Hayes, Robert Lauriston, Microx, Marty Sarussi, Carsten Schmidt,** and **Earl Vickers**. Thanks to the **ASJA Contract Watch** in the **Byline Conference** on The WELL.

The list goes on and I thank the following for their time, tips, advice, permissions, and assistance: **Tom Abate, John Perry Barlow, Anne Wells Branscomb, Pierre Cabanne, Steve Cisler, Robert Descharnes, Linda Garcia, A.M. Hammacher, Ben Hopper, Steve Johnson, The Knightmare, KPFA Archives, Bruce Lehman, Harold Lehman, Marco Livingstone, Richard Maulsby, John Milner, Colleen Muller, Nicholas Negroponte, Scott Nicholas, Rapid Lasergraphics,** and **Art Rogers.** Special acknowledgment to the **Painting Department at Butterfield & Butterfield Auctioneers**.

No major effort like this would succeed without the loving encouragement of my family and family of special friends. For their many hours of musing with me about the Net: thank you **Laura Scheflow** and **Allison Smith**. For your humor when I was sweating bullets, thank you, Dad, **Norman H. Carter**. And thanks to **Fortney, Evan** and **Graham Carter**—the whole family is online. Thanks to my **Aunt Bea** for always being there. And thank you, my husband, partner, technical support, and great love, **Gary W. Priester**.

Mary E. Carter

June 1996
Black Point, California

P.S. One final indulgence: To my **Chickens** on the Electronic Highway, the hens who provided me with the inspiration to go online. Proof that what goes 'round, comes 'round. Thanks girls!

Foreword

Artists are free spirits. I know, sometimes it doesn't feel that way. Nevertheless, I stand on my statement: artists are free spirits. You have to be, because we entrust you with (and punish you for) stretching our societal limits.

With that freedom comes responsibility. You must recognize those limits, judge which of them need to be stretched, and then shove them as hard as you can. But you also have to recognize which of them serve valid purposes, and work to protect and preserve them. That's hard work for a free spirit.

Copyright is, in my opinion as a non-artist, worth preserving and protecting. It's through copyright that the work of artists obtains money value. And even if you don't think money value is important, it's what makes it possible for you to buy paint or clay or a camera or a scanner, and to sell your work. It's society's medium of exchange between artist and buyer.

If it weren't for copyright, anyone could take your work, reproduce it, and pay you nothing for the time and energy and imagination that you invested in it.

In this book, Mary Carter explores how copyright protects your rights and those of other artists. She explains, with clarity and humor, an area of law that many artists avoid. And that's understandable, because the law was written by lawyers for what often seems to be the best of lawyer reasons: to make it necessary for an artist to call a lawyer at least monthly, if not daily, to find out what's legal. Mary's book (which I reviewed, edited, and contributed to from the perspective of a lawyer who's worked with artists for many years) should make it possible for you to avoid those calls most of the time, and to decide when the call can't be avoided.

With the advent of digitizing devices and revolutionary ways to publish your work, it's tempting to scan, edit, and post what intrigues you—and never ask permission. Mary's book tells why that's a bad idea. As someone who advises and counsels artists, I agree that it's a bad idea. But Mary and I both know that unless we offer alternatives that work, the bad idea will rule the world. So that's what this book offers: a lucid explanation of what the law is, why it's the way it is, and how to accomplish what your creative drive leads you to do without doing anything bad or illegal. Give it a try.

Brad Bunnin
Berkeley, California

CONTENTS

chapter one

INTRODUCTION

Origins of a Chicken Lady

I first became interested in copyright on the electronic superhighway when I started posting a regular topic online on The WELL, a virtual community and conferencing system based in Sausalito, California. By the marvelous serendipity of the online experience, and with the support of a whole group of online friends, my "Chickens Helping the Hungry" topic grew into a regular column. Like a newspaper columnist, I used the fulcrum of my topic to write about my views on all kinds of things, from the news of the day to the antics of my flock. I got to be known as The Chicken Lady on the WELL.

As the topic grew and my postings mounted into a book-length series of online articles, I began to wonder what would happen if someone, somewhere on the net, downloaded them and published them, for what I imagined would be (in a sort of gnawing paranoia) fame and fortune. The WELL has a proviso on the first screen that you see when you go online which states:

> You own your own words. This means that you are responsible for the words that you post on the WELL and that reproduction of those words without your permission in any medium outside the WELL's conferencing system may be challenged by you, the author.

But even thus assured, I was still not sure that my words would be truly safe from misuse if, for instance, some unscrupulous person on the other side of the globe took them for profit.

I am also an illustrator and graphic designer, using the medium of the computer to create my images. As the work goes out on disk, I often wonder about the actual control that I have over the usage of my images. What if one of my clients asked me to sign a contract giving them the right to use one of my illustrations on their Web page? Fine, okay. We agree to a use fee for this purpose. I'm satisfied they have paid me a fair compensation for this usage. They put my illustration into the landscape of the electronic superhighway. How do I know it stays on my client's Web page and none other? What if I discover that the site containing my illustration is linked to 15 other sites? Should I be paid for usage in those additional sites? Or is a link something different than a copy? And what about the naive infringer who downloads my image and uses it in his work? Or the lurker who downloads my image to just have in her personal files? Or the unscrupulous infringer who downloads it, makes posters, and sells them? Oh boy. This gets complicated. Sure, I have copyright law on my side. But, realistically, how am I going to enforce my rights? Realistically, I may never actually know if my copyrights have been infringed.

Since digital art moves in a swifter and more malleable medium than other forms of artwork, a whole new train of thought, and fear, has made me a "chicken lady" in more than just one sense of the word.

Who Owns What?
And What Can They Do About It?

In this era of computer generated graphic design, illustration, multimedia presentations, and photo manipulation, the issue of Who Owns What is critical to the individual computer artist. So is the issue of What Can They Do About It?

This new thing, the Internet, consists of hundreds of thousands of linked computer terminals. Each individual computer can send and receive digital information—text and images—via the phone lines. And individual computer users can also link their own words and images with any of the millions of other computer users' words and images. Using this network, it is now possible for people to access countless images. It's easy—perhaps too easy—to download any of these images to look at or to use. But is it ethical or legal to do so?

In this confusing plenitude, how does an illustrator know if the image—or the part of an image—she uses in an illustration is owned by someone else? How does a multimedia creator know if the film clip he decides to use in a QuickTime movie is in the public domain? Should the multimedia artist obtain a license to use any such film clips? Can a digital artist use any scanned image in an original work as long as he alters it enough? How do you copyright your original, digitally produced artwork? What if some other digital artist uses your digital art in their work? Should you promote your work on CD-ROM? Should you promote your work online on the electronic superhighway? How do you monitor usage of your images once they move into cyberspace? Who owns the work I produce while I am employed by a design firm or advertising agency? And the biggest question of the electronic information era: What if I get ripped off? This book is for the artist who does not want to become a victim of, or an unwitting accessory to, electronic highway robbery.

To simplify, the two fundamental issues are:

1. The copyright laws

2. Enforcing them

The first is a matter of record. The second is a matter of logistics. Never before has such a large audience, potentially hundreds of millions, had access to an artist's product. Never before has an individual artist had access to so many images. It is by far the easier task to read and understand the laws, than to enforce them, as an individual artist. If your copyright is being infringed and you never find out about it, are you nonetheless being damaged by the infringement? And if you do find out about it, will you be able to enforce the laws which were designed to protect you and your copyrights?

These are some of the issues that will be addressed in the following chapters. But before I dive into the fray I would like to address one other important issue for artists in the digital era.

How Can I Be a Free Spirited Artist and a Hardheaded Business Person?

There is a portion of the art community that holds that art is not a business. That it is something coming strictly from the soul. Something ineffable. Spiritual. And, in its creation, I, too, believe that the work flows through the artist in a mysterious and visionary process. But the moment an artist offers artwork for sale, whether it be in the heady enclaves of the fine art gallery, or the more temporal hallways of the advertising agency, the artist enters the realm of business. Any art proffered for money—to pay the rent, to buy the food, to purchase supplies—becomes product. And the artist with a product must, of necessity, know the ways of the marketplace. Opting out of this responsibility will result in disaster for the artist because, clearly, the marketplace is home to the arbiters of power.

I believe that knowing and understanding basic business law, contracts and copyrights, simple accounting skills, and commonsense business ethics will actually release an artist from stifling worries and conflicts. If you are being challenged on copyright infringement, for instance, precious creative energy can be eaten up in legal processes. If you have "signed your life away" in a contract you will kick yourself around the block. Life is hard enough for the artist, remuneration hard enough won. You do not need the added drain of these kinds of troubles. It is easier to be prepared. Learn the basics of your business as an artist. And retain that free spirit, uncluttered by business worries.

What This Book Is Not

This is not a definitive law textbook. It is not filled with all of the fine details of case law. It is, rather, a general reference, a useful guide to the issues in and around copyright law for visual artists in cyberspace. It will be, for many, a primer on the subject. For the subject of copyright is vast, complicated, hotly debated and, at this point, in flux. This book is not the last word. There will not be a last word on copyright on the net for many years to come.

ON THE OTHER HAND...

My Alter Ego Speaks Out.

As I worked on this book, I began writing a journal of my thoughts alongside the body of the text. In my journal I let go of the restrictions of reason and law and the issues and just let my right brain have a go at writing some words. After a while I noticed that these journal entries were valuable asides to the subject of copyright and held within them the kinds of thoughts that an artist would have while reading a book about the law. So I decided to include these journal entries here.

I have placed these asides throughout my text at points where I stopped and examined the "other hand" of an issue. These notes are as much a part of the story of copyright on the electronic superhighway as the actual laws, because they are the ambiguities, the gray areas, the subtleties which cannot be covered by a flat statement of law, section, and footnote.

So What's It All About?

This is a book about speed, pixels, and webs; murky gray areas and bright new lights; creators, creativity and technique; laws and lawlessness; the good, the bad, and the enforceable; hackers, software, and hard facts; the artist set among the philistines; and operating slightly out of control. It's about cruising down the electronic superhighway and avoiding highway robbery. One artist's shaky attempt to sort it all out before getting too badly sideswiped.

Terms and Definitions

Throughout this text I use a number of terms to refer to the global network of millions of computer terminals that are linked by satellite, cable, and phone lines: cyberspace, information superhighway, the Internet, the Net, the World Wide Web, the Web, etc. Even more broadly, various forms of digital information, reduced to the essence of 0's and 1's, can also travel point-to-point on dedicated fax lines, by so-called "sneaker net" on diskettes, Syquest disks, CD-ROMs, and video tapes, etc. For the purposes of this book, any digital information that moves from person to person by any of these means is considered to be traveling on the electronic superhighway.

COPYING AND COPYRIGHT LAW

Just put a circle C on it.

You are a commercial illustrator. For years you worked in airbrush, doing a super realistic style of work. Toasters, cars, people. You produced advertising illustration for major national advertisers. Gradually you have been honing your technique using photo manipulation and paint software and, painstakingly, you have converted your whole portfolio to a marketable digital art form. You place your work on CD-ROM and take it to your annual Society of Illustrators "Show Your Portfolio" meeting. There is quite a crowd here tonight and you are justifiably a bit nervous about your segment of the program. Will they like the new work?

But before the show-and-tell portion of the meeting, the vice president of technology raises a couple of questions before the attendees: Should copyrights be enforced on the electronic superhighway? And how should we, as artists, define copyright infringement, now that we're in the digital era?

You have been pretty indifferent to these subjects, if you even gave them a moment's thought. You've been too busy perfecting the mechanics of your new art form. So you are surprised to discover that, within minutes, the whole room is embroiled in a shouting match. One "camp" thinks copyright should be abandoned, that it stifles creativity with the new technology, and anyway it's just too hard to enforce in the digital era. Another believes that copyrights should, if anything, be made even stronger to withstand the onslaught of reckless copying that has been going on now that everyone is online. A vociferous contingent wants all copying banned and strong warning labels for scanners and screen capture software. Hecklers in the back shout, "Give up! Anyone can copy anything!"

It used to be, all you had to worry about was just signing your work and placing the copyright notice on it. Now that is only the beginning. In today's digital world, an artist must, at least, know the basics of copyright law. And an artist must understand what, exactly, copying is in a digital world. Only then can he or she can enter into the debate with an educated point of view. So here we go, into the breach. First: what is copying? Then: the basics of copyright law.

chapter one

A SHORT HISTORY OF COPYING

1895

The Long Gallery at the Louvre. A student has set up an easel, small stool, and paint box in front of Elisabeth Le Brun's painting Self Portrait with Daughter. The oily disarray of the paint box, casein oil, and scruffy, cheap paintbrushes and, indeed, of the student's smock, beret, and threadbare clothing stand in poignant contrast to the magnificent copy on which the student is working. The admiring visitors this day to the Louvre nod and whisper among themselves, feeling both excited at being able to watch this talented student at work and reluctant to break the spell of this moment of creation. The painting, glowing with the deft touch of the student's skills, rests against the rickety easel, and the viewers note that it is being painted in about two-thirds of the scale of the more famous painting it emulates.

This is as it has been for several generations now. Students at the Louvre are allowed to paint exact copies of famous paintings as long as they adhere to strict size limitations. In this way, perhaps, dealers or potential buyers will be warned off a substantial and uninformed investment should the painting come onto the market. And the painting probably will come onto the market, because the student needs the money. But buyers will know that this painting was produced by a student who made this copy to learn the technique of the masters and is not, even though masterful in and of itself, one of the great master's works.

Let's Talk Copying

If we're going to discuss copying and copyright law in terms of today's artists and their copying tools, then we have to look at copying in its historical context. Going back just one hundred years, examples of copying abound in both fine and commercial arts. Artists have a long and rich history of copying one another and of copying what they see around them. Their motives are interesting in relation to copyright laws because, for one reason or another, artists will copy. In the examples that follow I present a brief history of copying.

Infatuation?

In the example at the beginning of this chapter, we saw the student copying the work of the master. I remember being an art student. I remember falling in love with Van Gogh's paintings when I was nine years old, standing as close as I possibly could to his iris painting, entranced, teary, compelled, as other museum visitors jostled me, in what was probably my first adult reaction to a work of art. By the time I was about fourteen, I had my first oil painting box, that piney, oily wooden box that wafted turpentine when I opened the lid. And, of course I started painting copies of Van Gogh pictures. Rapturously I read his letters and languished in the sad melancholy hopelessness, the rather glamorous world (or so I believed, sitting in my middle-class home in the San Fernando Valley of the 1950s) of the suffering artist. I was in love. This may be a self-indulgent way of saying I believe every art student falls "in love" with an earlier artist, taking the emulation as far as copying the works of the historic and mythic predecessor.

But in addition to love, the young artist is learning craft. Learning to see. Learning to convert everyday scenery into a vision. Learning to conceptualize objects. Learning to think and translate thought into images. Most young artists go through a period of time when they copy, first the literal works of the mentor-artist, then the style of that, or other artists. My own then-favorite painter, Van Gogh, passed through such a stage of copying. He created many works in the style of Millet and fancied himself a kind of social commentator of his time, speaking to the humble integrity of the peasant and his potatoes.

And then, gradually and with a vivid passage, the young artist has a "breakthrough" and starts to paint differently from that first love. The young artist might start painting in yet another artist's style, but gradually, through a series of such breaks with the past, the artist reaches his or her own vision and the work starts to look like no work that came before. And then the copying ceases.

1916–1919. Parody?
The Lips on Everybody's Lips

And then the copying ceases. Unless you make copying your concept.

Around 1914, Marcel Duchamp started to display what he would later name his Readymades. A selection of found objects gleaned from the detritus of early industrial production line merchandise. A galvanized bottle rack. A bicycle wheel. A hat rack, dangling from the ceiling, immortalized.

While you cannot call this "copying," exactly, it might be a sort of "appropriation" (sound familiar?), a setting apart of mundane manufactured objects from their natural context. Now both the artist and the viewer can see them apart from their homely functionality. Look. This thing looks different when you put it in the plain white shell of the gallery.

Then Duchamp started a process of "Rectifications" on his culled Readymades. In 1919 Duchamp took an advertisement for Sapolin Enamel and added a few touches of his own—to do what? To make a biting satire of the sentimental little ad? To be obtuse? To flag the advertiser's blatant use of a little girl to sell enamel?

ON THE OTHER HAND...

This image really begs the question: what if you did something like this today? Bringing it into today's world: what if you put a mustache on a poster of one of Andrew Wyeth's Helga paintings? Unless there's some legal justification for what you did, you've copied—and you've infringed. There is also the possibility that you might be infringing Helga's right of privacy by appropriating her image for commercial purposes. And all you wanted to do was create a nice biting piece of parody! Well, if you succeeded, you may have a valid defense against an infringement claim. We'll consider whether you do later on. 🐂

Then there is the image on everybody's lips. This next famous "copy," by Duchamp, was mentioned by several of the attorneys I spoke with in the course of researching this book. This image is the first line of defense by those who seek a precedent for copying. Duchamp's Mona Lisa with a mustache (see page 219). Assembled in 1919, the image is titled *L.H.O.O.Q. (Elle a chaud au cul)* and is the most famous of his Rectified Readymades, consisting of pencil on a reproduction of the Mona Lisa.

1869. 1949. 1969. Iconographer or Iconoclast?

The artist as an iconographer is one who creates artworks with reference to conventional meanings in objects or images. The artist as an iconoclast is the breaker or destroyer of conventional images and meanings.

In 1869 Manet painted *The Balcony*, a familiar Impressionist icon of bourgeois Parisians sitting on a balcony

(Figure 2 in Appendix I). In his 1949 painting called *Perspective: The Balcony by Manet,* Magritte copied the painting, replacing the figures with coffins (Figure 3). What is going on here? Is the artist intentionally defacing these original images to shock us? To mock? To make us laugh? Or cry? Is Magritte serious or heretical? Metaphorical or satirical? Clever and iconoclastic? Or just too lazy to come up with his own imagery?

The 1960s: Vox Populi

The '60s Pop Art movement gives us memorable examples of copying. Punchy and heroic images, copied every which way from Sunday. Everyday objects made monumentally huge. Or repeated, copied over and over and over, in a texture of monotony. Or defaced and dismembered, juxtaposed with other copies. Popular icons reexamined and made into more than the sum of their parts. Art that copied the lives of everyday people, objects, artifacts, events.

It may have begun with Jasper Johns in his 1955 painting *Flag.* A copy of the stars and stripes. What was once sacrosanct was now subject matter. Was this an editorial comment? Political satire? Was it okay to do this? Was it art?

The dam burst loose. It was every man for himself. And most of the artists of the Pop movement were men. Next thing you know Peter Blake paints *On The Balcony* in 1955–57 with more allusions to the famous Manet picture. Only in this painting Blake copies and arranges a pastiche of images taken from twentieth-century magazines. Products, logos, picture postcards, buttons, popular photography, and newspaper clippings.

At the same time Richard Hamilton makes a collage called *Just What Is It That Makes Today's Homes So Different, So Appealing?* He clips out advertising images from popular magazines—sofas, musclemen, sexy women, housewives. Your Hoover. Your Ford logo. Your ham.

Then Peter Blake copied the faces of the heroes of the period in his enamel, photo collage, and record assemblage called *Got a Girl*, done in 1960–61. Ricky Nelson, Fabian, Elvis. Elvis again. Frankie Avalon, Bobby Rydell. I just have to ask: did the law require that he get permission to use these famous faces from their agents? Nowadays, to be safe, you would have to obtain permission or risk a lawsuit for breach of a celebrity's right of publicity, although if your artwork is a piece of fine art (as distinguished, say, from a $10 poster destined for dorm room walls), there's a good chance you wouldn't need permission.

When You Don't Have Arms or a Head, It's Hard to Defend Yourself

Poor, beleaguered Victory of Samothrace, noblest of Greek statues and suddenly she's just an artist's punching bag. And you can't say much more for her sister, the armless Venus de Milo and her winsome younger cousin, Botticelli's Venus. As Pop Art matured, it ranged throughout culture and history, gobbling up images, copying them and reinventing them. And, just an aside here: that much-copied Venus later became the logo-lady on a very famous and familiar piece of software for illustrators.

In 1962 Yves Klein painted a plaster reproduction of the Victory of Samothrace a vivid ultramarine blue, taking the classical icon and refurbishing it. Now it becomes yet another icon, cloaked in a coat of something quite unexpected.

But it was not only the Pop artists who copied and manipulated icons. The earlier Surrealist, Salvador Dalí, copied the Venus de Milo in at least two of his works, most memorable of which is his *Venus de Milo With Drawers*, a plaster sculpture Dalí created in 1936. In fact, Dalí simply marked where the drawers should be on the famous statue, and Marcel Duchamp, copyist extraordinaire, made the model.

Later, in 1968–70, Dalí again copied the Venus in his painting *The Hallucinogenic Toreador*. The painting contains many images in it, including illustrative elements and items from popular culture of the time. The painting is not unlike some of the imagery you see today, created with scanned images and photo-manipulation software. But today, the artist might have to obtain the license to use some of the images which, in Dalí's time, were considered to be a part of the artist's natural world of visual resources.

Is Nothing Sacred, Mickey?

Copying attained further legitimacy with the rapid development and further evolution of the Pop Art movement. Paintings, serigraphs, collages, and sculpture containing copied elements appeared in galleries and museums, apparently sanctioned by the critics and historians, as "genuine" objects of expression. In his stunning book, *Pop Art: A Continuing History*, Marco Livingstone observed:

> *It seemed indifferent and even hostile to passionately held views on uniqueness, artistic personality and originality: invention was being replaced by shameless copying from existing sources.*

Now such artists as Tom Wesselmann, Ed Rushcha, Mel Ramos, Roy Lichtenstein, and, of course, Andy Warhol were using brand-name products and brand-name cartoon characters in their work. Coca-Cola, Campbell's Soup, Budweiser, Tareyton cigarettes, Mars Bars, and

Standard Oil. Orphan Annie, Superman, Popeye, and Mickey Mouse. All of the popular icons of the era became fodder for the work.

In fact, the use of existing cartoon characters in fine art continued into the 1980s. As far as copyright infringement in these cases, it seems that as long as the poor artist was a virtual unknown, he did not have an infringement problem. But as soon as the artist got to be "known" the cartoon copyright holders came down on him. Some of these cartoon copyists were issued "cease and desist" orders or asked to alter the cartoon characters so that they could not be recognized. In some cases, the artists were granted limited licenses to use the images on single fine-art objects.

Faces, Faces, Faces

And it was not just inanimate products and animated cartoons that were blatantly copied. The Pop artists copied faces, all kinds of faces, from the Kennedys to the men on the most wanted posters. Mona Lisa made her comeback again and again and again, in Andy Warhol's appropriately titled *Mona Lisa*. Even the artifacts of our nation's war casualties were copied as subject matter for fine art, as seen in the reproduction of the statue of soldiers raising the flag at Iwo Jima in Ed Kienholz's *The Portable War Memorial*. Nothing was too sacred, too profane, or too banal to copy, rearrange, and reconstitute in this new art form. Is this kind of art satire? Parody? Appropriation or misappropriation?

Did the Pop Artists Get Popped?

With this rampaging copying, did anyone get sued? It was a mixed bag. Some Pop artists escaped accusations of infringement. Roy Lichtenstein, Tom Wesselman,

James Rosenquist, Claes Oldenberg, and Jasper Johns—
all of whom appropriated cultural icons and images—
were never sued for copyright infringement. But Robert
Rauschenberg and Andy Warhol were sued. Since they
settled out of court, there was virtually no publicity about
their cases. So what's the difference between those
artists who were sued for their appropriations and those
artists who were not?

It comes to this: when an artist copied an image into a
single painting, for instance, the courts seemed to consider the use permissible. But when an artist created
multiples, as in a suite of prints, then he might have
copyright problems, unless he could convince a judge
that the use was parody.

The Homage: What Happened to "After"?

Throughout the history of contemporary art movements,
there has been yet another tradition of copying. Similar
to the young artist's love affair with a mentor-artist where
she copies the work is the homage to the more mature
artist. In this kind of work the artist copies or transforms
either a composition or a concept from the work of a
favorite earlier artist. The copying artist gives the work
a title like: *Such and Such a Work, after Manet*, meaning the work was inspired by another artist. The viewer
is supposed to be as much concerned with the original
work of art as with this later artist's interpretation of the
work. The homage is just that, an appreciation or
acknowledgment of one artist's work by another artist.
Examples of such works are Patrick Caulfield's *Greece
Expiring on the Ruins of Missolonghi, after Delacroix*;
Rupert Garcia's *Magritte Remembered*; and this excep-
tional example of an homage by Salvador Dalí painted
in 1933 and titled *Gala and the Angelus of Millet
Immediately Preceding the Arrival of the Conic Anamor-
phosis*. Of this painting, Dalí said:

In June 1932, there suddenly came to my mind without any close or conscious association, which would have provided an immediate explanation, the image of The Angelus of Millet. This image consisted of a visual representation which was very clear and in colors. It was nearly instantaneous and was not followed by other images. It made a very great impression on me, and was most upsetting to me because, although in my vision of the afore-mentioned image everything corresponded exactly to the reproductions of the picture with which I was familiar, it appeared to me nevertheless absolutely modified and charged with such latent intentionality that The Angeles of Millet "suddenly" became for me the pictorial work which was the most troubling, the most enigmatic, the most dense and the richest in unconscious thoughts that I had ever seen.

What more can I say? It's just how the artist's mind works. You see. You glean from every visual, new and known. You draw. You draw from the work of others. It is what artists have done and will do, regardless, I believe, of copyright laws that aim to harness this form of derivative imaging. But there are limits, and they've severely restricted the artist's right to appropriate anything, for any purpose, that her creative instincts led her to create. We'll be taking a sharp look at those limits.

Then Again, He Did if For Money

Then there is this motivator: money. Among the boldest of the copiers has to be J.S.G. Boggs. He doesn't just appropriate parts or rearrange wholes, he copies dollar bills. And tens. And hundreds. Now, clearly, his is not a copyright case, but whether or not it is a forgery case depends upon your viewpoint. Unlike the crafty forger, Boggs sits right down in a restauraunt, tells the maître d' what he's up to and asks if he can pay for his dinner (and let's assume he adds a nice gratuity) using his exquisite copies. Generally, the answer is yes. After all, this guy is good for business. It's good PR. Has he had any trouble over his crafty counterfeits? You bet. The Secret Service, with its diminished sense of humor, is not amused. They recently searched and seized about a hundred drawings and paintings from Boggs' apartment. But, apparently, Boggs is quite a hit in Europe and Australia where his works are declared to be "art" by the courts. So here's a case where an artist copied for his supper. And isn't the point "money," after all? Whether it's how to meet the rent on the studio, how to negotiate use fees, how to hit it big, money is the artwork you can never get enough of. Unless you're J.S.G. Boggs.

Art for Commerce: The Comprehensive Art Form

Meanwhile, across town and in 1969, in the hallways of American advertising agencies, yet another kind of artist does yet another kind of copying. It's the late '60s, the heyday of Madison Avenue's hold on the art of commerce. Advertising illustrators, graphic designers, and advertising agency art directors copy works of the masters, of various fine arts movements, of photographers, of illustrators, and of each other. All commercial artists of that era collected vast "scrap" files of photographs torn from magazines, newspapers, from artist's promotional pieces, from anything printed that they could get their hands on so that they would have the images they needed when they put together a "comprehensive" layout. Comps were pieced together for every kind of advertiser—for cars, toothpaste, pet food, fast food—to show the clients how an ad would look once it was produced.

In the '60s and '70s art directors at large national advertising agencies cut pictures out of magazines and traced them in the Lucigraph to make a "comp" of a magazine ad. The art director of that era then added his client's logo and filled in color using Magic Markers. He sent the layout to the stat house and used the final Photostat of the composed elements to sell the layout to his client. The process still goes on today. Only the technology is much more sophisticated.

Today, an art director at a large national advertising agency prepares a layout for a magazine ad. She wants to show her clients how their food product would look in a particular photographic style. She goes over to her file of photographer's self-promotional CD-ROMs and finds the sample of the photographer's work she wants to use. Then she scans in a photograph, from a magazine, of a serving of her client's type of food product, the work of yet another photographer, and uses a popular photo-manipulation program to enhance her "new" image. She then obtains color output and presents it to her client as her comprehensive layout.

Why All the Attention to Copying Now?

The history of copying in fine and commercial art is a long one. Sometimes copying is seen as part of the noble tradition of learning. When a student copies a painting, a certain amount of good faith is taken for granted. Sometimes copying has taken the form of a parody, as, in the work of the Pop movement of the '60s and other art forms. And sometimes copying has been an expedient, as in the case of the advertising industry; in a world where image is all important, how better for an art director to sell an idea to a client?

The practice of copying in the arts is a long one. But never before has copying been so newsworthy. The current state of high anxiety and media attention around copyright law hinges on three important technological changes:

- Digital images can travel very great distances from their originators, leaving few tracks.

- Digitally transmitted images can produce an excellent "file" that may be effectively reproduced and sold.

- Digital images are much easier to change, in dramatic ways, than hard copy.

For artists, it's a whole new world. These changes have radically unbalanced the way copying functions in the digital era. Suddenly, art can be posted to and grabbed from places like the World Wide Web or CD-ROMs, by anyone, easily and without any reduction in quality. Suddenly the potential number of copyists has jumped exponentially. And just as suddenly, such misappropriations have become harder to catch. We are not just talking good old traditional copying here. We are talking about the fact that images may be copied and marketed as never before. A world away from the original artist's studio. A copied image can hit the artist where she lives—in the pocketbook—over and over again. Before we can fully assess this problem and possible remedies, we need to look at the legal framework for all this: the Copyright Law itself.

FOR WHAT IT's WORTH...

Books

The Brothers Duchamp
By Pierre Cabanne
Little, Brown & Company
1271 Avenue of the Americas
New York, NY 10020
ISBN 0-8212-0666-4

This is one of those wonderful big art books, with plenty of color pictures and a wealth of historical information about the unique vision of Marcel Duchamp, who may well have been the father of parody in the fine-art world.

Pop Art: A Continuing History
By Marco Livingstone
Harry N. Abrams, Inc.
100 Fifth Avenue
New York, NY 10011
ISBN 0-8109-3770-77

This is a big book, absolutely loaded with Pop images, and almost every page contains artworks with some form of copying in them—from logos, to products, to famous faces, to previous artworks. The accompanying text is very detailed and tracks the history of the Pop movement.

The Studios of Paris: The Capital of Art in the Late Nineteenth Century
By John Milner
Yale University Press
302 Temple Street
New Haven, CT 06511
ISBN 0-300-04749-5

A large paperback picture book that shows and describes the life of the artist in the late nineteenth-century Paris art scene. This book starts off by exploring the topic of student artists copying paintings in the Louvre and provides further insight into why these artists copied.

Magritte
By A. M. Hammacher
Harry N. Abrams, Inc.
100 Fifth Avenue
New York, NY 10011
ISBN 0-8109-0278-8

The works of Magritte are filled with visual references to other artists' works and are well worth studying in terms of today's fair use doctrine, which is discussed in more detail in Chapter 3.

Dalí
By Robert Descharnes
Harry N. Abrams, Inc.
100 Fifth Avenue
New York, NY 10011
ISBN 0-8109-0830-1

Dalí "copied" many famous artworks in the course of exploring his subconscious creative terrain. But, even in terms of today's copyright laws, his work would be judged to be acceptable under fair use. To discover why, take a good long look at some of the works included in this book.

California Painters: New Work
By Henry T. Hopkins and Jim McHugh
Chronicle Books
275 Fifth Street
San Francisco, CA 94103
ISBN 0-87701-593-7
Copying in fine art continues right up to the most recent art movements. This book includes contemporary paintings with many "copied" or derivative elements from the works of other painters. Created by such diverse artists as Alexis Smith, Jess, and Rupert Garcia, these paintings demonstrate that copying, in one form or another, continues yet today.

Periodicals

ARTnews Magazine
ARTnews Subscription Service
P.O. Box 56590
Boulder, CO 80322-6590
Or call: 800/284-4625
$32.95 per year

One of the best magazines covering the current fine-art scene. Not too precious for the average reader, yet meaty and informative for the professional fine or graphic artist.

Communication Arts Magazine
P.O. Box 10300
410 Sherman Avenue
Palo Alto, CA 94303
$50.00 per year

The sine qua non of graphic design magazines, CA always features the best in the field. Tad Crawford's regular column is a great source of copyright information.

HOW Magazine
P.O. Box 5250
Harlan, IA 51593-0750
Or call: 800/333-1115
$49.00 per year

An excellent magazine that features how-to articles for the graphic designer and commercial artist. From production tips, to accounting, to current copyright information, this magazine provides a lot of solid information.

Publish Magazine
Subscriber Services
P.O. Box 5039
Brentwood, TN 37024
Or call: 800/656-7495
$39.90 per year

This is the magazine for the computer graphic design and art professional. Focusing on a wide range of issues in the digital era, it provides monthly in-depth analyses of industry issues—from business to production to copyrights.

PC Magazine
P.O. Box 54093
Boulder, CO 80322-4093
Or call: 800/289-0429
$49.97 per year

The source magazine for the latest hardware and software for PC systems.

Online

The ads conference at the WELL
This conference on the WELL is worth the membership if you are looking for a discussion forum on advertising. People in this conference are in the business and discuss the meaning of the Net, sometimes very heatedly, from a marketing perspective.

The eff (Electronic Frontier Foundation) conference at the WELL
Hosted by founding members of the Electronic Frontier Foundation, this conference frequently ranges over copyrights in the digital era, and much archived discussion is available on the topic. Sometimes there is more opinion than fact, but discussion is always thought provoking. (Note: you can find the Electronic Frontier Foundation on the Web at www.eff.org.)

chapter two

COPYRIGHT LAW. THE PLAIN ENGLISH VERSION

The Constitutional Framework for Copyright Law

Today's copyright laws have their roots in English common law and in the U.S. Constitution. Our copyright statutes were put into place to encourage the development of intellectual property in the form of scientific and artistic products for the public good. Creators of original artistic or scientific works are given exclusive rights for limited times to copy and distribute their works. The Constitutional framework supports the concept that creators may control the use of and seek payment for their original creations and for their derivative works. That concept is the essence of copyright law. It's what makes possible the whole economic structure of the art world and the publishing world and the software world.

Your Artwork Is Your Property

The term "intellectual property" refers to a special kind of property that has value because it can be reproduced from an original. Intellectual property includes artwork, photography, photos that have been digitally altered using photo-manipulation software, multimedia productions, and a whole range of other types of property (such as software, for instance). Some of it is covered by copyright law; some is protected by other laws, such as trademark, trade secret, and unfair competition law, which we won't cover here. Don't let anyone tell you that intellectual property is any less real or any less deserving of protection than other forms of property. The law protects the rights of those who own intellectual property in a big way.

Your art becomes protected by copyright when you take it from idea or concept to something in fixed and tangible form. Some have argued that digital and digitized art passes through a period of being somewhat intangible as pure information, that is, when it is in digital form, a series of 0s and 1s. But the law disagrees; at this point, even in its digital form as 0s and 1s—on disk or CD, film or printed on paper, T-shirts, tote bags, magazine advertisements, brochures, swizzle sticks, you name it—it's protected property. It can be licensed or sold outright by its owner.

When a manufacturer makes shoes, she learns her trade, becomes a skilled worker, makes an investment in capital equipment to produce the shoes, purchases raw materials for making the shoes, determines price based on market conditions and the quality of her product, and sells the shoes to willing buyers. If her warehouse is broken into and shoes are stolen, she has the law to support her in prosecuting those who stole her property.

So, too, the artist learns her trade, becomes a skilled worker, makes an investment in capital equipment to make art, purchases raw materials for making the art, determines price based on market conditions and the quality of the art, and sells art to willing buyers. If her digital files are broken into and images are stolen, she has the law to support her in prosecuting those who stole her property.

Do not be confused by the term intellectual property. Your artwork—once you've completed it—is tangible and fixed, and it's protectable intellectual property. It is viable as an object and, potentially, marketable as such, and reproductions of it are also marketable. Whether you create paintings, computer-generated illustrations, graphic design, logos, multimedia presentations, or a home page on the Web, your art, your property, can be protected by copyright laws.

What Can Be Protected by Copyright?

Section 102(a) of the Copyright Act states:

> *Copyright protection subsists...in original works of authorship fixed in any tangible medium of expression, now known or later developed, from which they can be perceived, reproduced, or otherwise communicated, either directly or with the aid of a machine or device.*

The basic requirements that a work of art must meet to qualify for copyright protection are that:

- **It must be original.** The artwork must be an original.

- **It must be creative.** The artwork must show at least a minimum amount of creativity.

- **It must be fixed in a tangible medium.** The artwork must be fixed in one of the tangible mediums listed in the next section.

Given the Above, Exactly Who Owns What?

You own your original. You own your creations and are entitled to the benefits of copyright protection for such fixed, tangible objects as:

- Your artwork in its digital state as 1s and 0s

- Your paintings and drawings

- Your lithographs, serigraphs, or other prints

- Sculpture and other tangible artistic (but not practical) objects

- Your photographs and photomontages

- Your montages or collages created out of cut and pasted elements

- Your montages or collages created out of your own original artwork or artwork for which you have received the license to copy

- Your original artwork that you have scanned into your computer

- Artwork you have created using bit-mapped or vector drawing, painting, or photo-manipulation programs or any combination of these digital media

- Your multimedia productions on videotape or film

- Your digital artwork created on a computer, including when it is in digital format of 0s and 1s

- Your digital artwork on diskette, CD-ROM or SyQuest disk, or any other file format

- Your digitized artwork (works created by you in traditional media and transferred to digital format for instance for a portfolio or self-promotional piece) on diskette, CD-ROM or SyQuest disk, or any other digital file format

- Your artwork uploaded to an online conferencing system or BBS or on the Wide World Web in digital format or graphically produced as bit-mapped or vector files

Though extensive, this list is certainly not complete. If you can see or touch your artwork, with or without the aid of a machine or device, no matter what its medium, it qualifies as being fixed in a tangible medium of expression. And you own it and the copyrights to it (unless you don't; see "Warning: Work for Hire Doesn't Belong to Its Creator" later in this chapter for what *work made for hire* means).

What Are My Rights as the Original Creator of a Work of Art?

You, as the creator and owner of an original work, are granted a bundle of rights under the Copyright Act. The rights are exclusive, which means that you, and only you, may use them, or allow others to use them. It's the exclusivity of copyright that makes it valuable to the artist.

The rights that make up that bundle of rights are separately licensable and enforceable as follows:

- **You have the exclusive right to reproduce your copyrighted work.** You can make as many copies of your original artwork as the market will bear: a limited edition of ten fine-art prints, say, or 10,000 posters. And you can prevent anyone else from reproducing copies of it. You can license the right to reproduce it to others.

What, Exactly, Is a Copy?

Funny you should ask. And it's not as dumb a question as it sounds. A lot of fine minds have devoted thousands of hours trying to define what is, *exactly*, a copy on the electronic superhighway. In addition to the usual copying media, which include every familiar tool from the pencil to the camera, we have many new digital tools for copying artworks in cyberspace. Scanners and screen-capture software are two of the most obvious tools for copying. But we could add to this list your computer's RAM memory, too. Or hard disk, for that matter.

So far, we can find at least one official definition of *a copy* in the digital era, and it comes to us in a 1995 government document titled *Intellectual Property and the National Information Infrastructure* (for brevity's sake, I'll call this document the White Paper. You may also see it referred to as the "Green Paper," because it was originally circulated for public comment in draft form with a green cover), issued by the Department of Commerce Information Infrastructure Task Force. Any interested citizen may obtain a copy of this document from the DOC offices in Washington, D.C. More about this document in Chapter 6.

ON THE OTHER HAND...

This is preposterous! As you can infer from this, the last time you netsurfed, you copied someone's copyrighted material. That merely looking at something on your screen might be put in the same category as real copying seems, on the face of it, impossibly overreaching. What is the difference between an average citizen thumbing through copyrighted works in a library and an average citizen "thumbing through" copyrighted works on the Web? This interpretation of "copying," in its strict wording and application, eradicates the concept of Web browsing. Or else makes infringers of us all. Surely, something has to give.

The White Paper defines copying as follows:

In each of the instances set out below, one or more copies is made:

- *When a work is placed into a computer, whether on a disk, diskette, ROM, or other storage device or in RAM for more than a very brief period, a copy is made.*

- *When a printed work is "scanned" into a digital file, a copy—the digital file itself—is made.*

- *When other works—including photographs, motion pictures, or sound recordings—are digitized, copies are made.*

- *Whenever a digitized file is "uploaded" from a user's computer to a bulletin board system or other server, a copy is made.*

- *Whenever a digitized file is "downloaded" from a BBS or other server, a copy is made.*

- *When a file is transferred from one computer network user to another, multiple copies are made.*

- *Under current technology, when a user's computer is being used as a "dumb" terminal to access a file resident on another computer such as a BBS or Internet host, a copy of the portion viewed is made in the user's computer. Without such copying into the RAM or buffer of the user's computer, no screen display would be possible. (White Paper, pp. 65–66)*

- **You have the exclusive right to prepare derivative works based on your copyrighted work.** You may modify your work and create something based on it. The modified version may be similar to the original (a mass-market poster greatly resembles an original photograph, for example). Or it may be very different (an animated cartoon goes way beyond a simple drawing, but it's nonetheless derived from it). Equally important, you may prevent others from creating something new but based on your work without your permission.

Quoting again from the White Paper:

> *A user who modifies—by annotating, editing, translating or otherwise significantly changing—the contents of a downloaded file creates a derivative work. (White Paper, p. 67)*

- **You have the exclusive right to distribute copies of your copyrighted work to the public by sale or other transfer of ownership, to prevent others from doing so, and to license others to do so.** For instance, you have the right to sell your posters and greeting cards to a distributor, or directly to a shop. On the electronic superhighway, the right to distribute your own work becomes very significant. You can post your work on the Web, which can be a useful medium for distribution and self-promotion for your artwork. And you have the legal right to prevent anyone else from posting your work without your consent. What's more, if you do post it, you can limit the right of others to use it.

- **You have the exclusive right to perform your copyrighted work publicly in the case of literary, musical, dramatic, and choreographic works, pantomimes, and motion pictures and other audiovisual works.** For instance, you may mount a performance at an art gallery, local community theater, or a school. Or, you may put your audiovisual work online, where those who log on can play it back for their pleasure.

- **You have the exclusive right to display your copyrighted work publicly in the case of literary, musical, dramatic, and choreographic works, pantomimes, and pictorial, graphic, or sculptural works, including individual images of a motion picture or other audiovisual**

work. For instance, you may display your work at an art gallery, in a shopping mall, or in a store. Or on the Net.

You can sell, or license, any or all of these rights, piece-meal or all together. In fact, it's the usual thing for photographers to license fewer than all rights to a magazine, or for a designer to specify that a given graphic design may be used only for a specified purpose. You then retain all of your other exclusive copyrights. Later on, you might license that same illustration for publication as a poster. Or you may create a derivative work from it by creating something new, based on that same illustration.

What about My Unpublished Works?

Copyright protection is available for both published and unpublished works. This means that the artworks in your studio or in storage, or works that you have not yet sold to anyone, receive the same copyright protection as the artworks you've sent out into the marketplace. A work is considered to be published once it is displayed, sold to a client, or performed in public. A work is considered to be unpublished if you have not displayed, sold, or performed the work in public.

What about My Copyrights on the Electronic Superhighway?

The simple answer is this: Legally, as of this writing, your basic copyrights stay in effect, even online, on the World Wide Web, and in any digital format.

This means that nobody may reproduce your work, create derivative works from your work, distribute your work, perform your work, or display your work without your express permission. For instance, users of an online service provider may not download one of your images and then copy your work to their hard drive without your permission. They may not download an image from the Net, or from a CD-ROM or from any other digital file, and then use a portion of it in their own artwork, without your permission. Just because it's easy to download images from locations on the electronic superhighway does not mean that you lose copyright protection. And in a way, this last statement is the key to this whole book: the new technology may make copyright infringement easier than it's ever been, and harder to detect, but unauthorized use is still copyright infringement.

ON THE OTHER HAND...

Some attorneys theorize that it may one day be held in a court of law that there is an implied license to copy when you put your artwork on the Net. According to the White Paper: "Under current technology, when a user's computer is being used...to access a file...a copy of at least the portion viewed is made in the user's computer." So artwork viewed online is routinely "copied." How is this any different from someone thumbing through books in a library? It may not be, if all the user does is view the copied file in transient memory. But if the user then copies the file to her hard disk, something else has happened, something that feels a lot like making an unauthorized reproduction. Then again, what if my images are "linked" to a zillion different World Wide Web sites? Shouldn't I receive a use fee for each and every link? Or is a link a copy in the first place? Hmmmm. This is not going to be simple. 🐂

Is Linking the Same as Copying?

One of the beauties of the World Wide Web is the feature called "linking," which lets you jump from one Web site to another with a single click on a word or a graphic image. At the moment there is spirited debate about whether creating a link from one site to another constitutes copying the contents of that other site. Some people say creating a link is the same as copying. Some say linking and copying are not the same. I shall present both sides here for your consideration. When you put up your Web pages, you should at least know the arguments, pro and con. Ultimately, this question will be decided in Congress or the courts.

When you put up your Web site, with all your wonderful graphics, others out on the Net may create a link to your Web site on their Web site. A link is created by programming a bit of HTML

(Hypertext Markup Language) so that a "hot spot" appears in either the text or graphics of the Web site. A Net surfer scans the Web pages with Netscape, for instance, observes the little grabbing fist icon, and knows that whatever the fist grabs onto is a link. By simply clicking on it, the Net surfer is transferred to the linked site. The link takes the Net surfer into a completely new Web site.

Does creating a link constitute a copy? First, let's look at the point of view that it does not.

The most common point of view is that links are just signposts or directional arrows that show you the way to something. The person who creates the link is simply saying, "This way for a cool site." Thus, a link is not a copy, but an instruction, a piece of advice, an arrow.

But Then Again, If It Looks like a Duck and Acts like a Duck, It's a Duck

Here is a hypothetical example of how creating a link is the same as creating a copy of the contents of the linked-to site. Let's say you have been hired to do an illustration for the *Chicago Tribune's* Web edition for an article entitled "The American Baby." You negotiate for a limited one-time usage of your illustration in the *Tribune's* Web edition. Then the *New York Time's* Web edition puts a link to the *Tribune's* Web site. For the Web user reading the *Times's* site, getting to the *Tribune's* site is so easy—just a click away—that the material on the *Tribune's* site is virtually included on the *Times's* site. The "effect" of that link is that your illustration is now available to the *Times's* readers as well as the *Tribune's*. Shouldn't you be paid for this expansion in the circulation of your illustration? Surely if the illustration were published in both hardcopy newspapers, you'd have no trouble convincing a court that the second paper had infringed your copyright.

Pro and Con Will Meet in the Courts

Have the courts defined copying on the Web? Has copyright law been amended to clarify the meaning of Web links? Not as of this writing. And, it bears repeating, the authors of the White Paper, struggling with the reach and intent of copyright law, observed that:

> *As more and more works are available primarily or exclusively* online, *it is critical that researchers, students and other members of the public have opportunities with the online equivalent to their current opportunities* off-line *to browse through copyrighted works in their schools and public libraries.* (White Paper, p. 133)

This approach makes sense, if it implies that some kinds of access are acceptable and others aren't, because that's the way the law works now. So the discussion of links must be done in the context of what happens to the linked material at the end of the linkage. Did the end viewer just look at the work? Or was the original artwork downloaded and made into T-shirts and postcards and sold for a profit? It's not too hard to decide which of these two uses ought to be an infringing use and which ought to be free of legal consequences. Just looking at a linked display, or even pointing the way to a cool site, should not constitute copyright infringement. But if the effect of the link might deprive an artist of a valid usage fee for a use the artist has the right to control, then the use ought to be treated as an infringement. So it's the end user's usage that should determine the potential for copyright infringement. If certain links "look like a duck and act like a duck," a court might find that it would be good social policy to treat them as "ducks." See you in court.

How Do I Get Copyright Protection?

You get copyright protection automatically on creation.
This is true even for works that are created on your computer, whether you keep them there or upload them onto the Net.

Registration is not necessary, but is highly recommended.
Yes, your work is automatically protected by copyright law, even if you do not file the official registration forms, but if there is an infringement, your day in court may be easier and more lucrative if you have registered your work. To begin with, you can't carry on your lawsuit if you haven't registered. And registration makes it much easier to prove that you own the copyright you're claiming, and that it began to apply to the work on the date you claim it did. Finally, you may be eligible for certain kinds of money damages and for reimbursement of attorney's fees if you've registered.

How to Register Your Copyrights

To register a work for copyright, first call the Forms Hotline at 202/707-9100 to obtain a copy of Form VA, the one for works of visual art. Complete the form according to the instructions attached to it (it's a very simple one) and attach the required copies (color prints, transparencies, code, and so on) of your artwork to the form. You may also register a group of unpublished works on one form. Then send the form, the copies of your image(s), and a $20 fee to: Register of Copyrights, Copyright Office, Library of Congress, Washington, DC 20559. Copyright registration goes into effect on the date that the form, the copies of the image(s), and the fee are received by the Copyright Office.

A copyright notice is not necessary, but is desirable.
A copyright notice looks like this: © Mary Carter 1996. If you like, you may use either the word *Copyright* or the strange abbreviation *copr.* instead of the ©, but the © is the worldwide symbol for copyright, so you should probably use it. The order isn't important, and there are

exceptions for certain artworks whose design would be impaired by a prominent copyright notice, but it's best to comply with the technical requirements and not get creative here. Place the copyright notice where people can readily see it. Make it large enough so that it can be easily read and recognized. If your work is likely to be distributed in Latin America, add these words: "All rights reserved."

How Long Do My Copyrights Last?

For the most part, your copyrighted work is protected for your lifetime plus 50 years. That's the general rule for work created on or after January 1, 1978. If your work is anonymous or pseudonymous, or was done as work made for hire, the protection lasts for a total of 75 years from its first publication, or 100 years from its creation, whichever is shorter. And yes, there's an exception: if an anonymous or pseudonymous author's identity is revealed during the term of copyright, the term changes to the life of the author plus 50 years. That's logical.

Works created before January 1, 1978, are subject to different rules. If the owner of one of those older copyrights does everything right, the total length of copyright protection is 75 years from the date the copyright was originally obtained.

When the term of protection expires, the work goes into the public domain, which simply means that copyright protection no longer applies, and no one needs permission, or must pay anything, for the right to use the work.

May I Sell the Rights to Copy My Work?

Yes. Such a sale is called a "license." It means that you give someone else permission to "infringe," to use your work in ways you agree to and describe. You may sell all of the rights to copy your work, or you may sell some of the rights, restricting the scope of the license in terms of duration, geographic scope, markets, media, and so on. For example, you may allow the license to run for the entire length of the copyright itself—your lifetime plus 50 years—or you may limit it to a few years. Or you might license the United States rights to one company and the Japanese rights to another. Or you might grant a magazine the right to publish your illustration once, then license the same illustration to a poster company for posters, mugs, and greeting cards, but for no other products.

Are There Any Other Protections for My Artwork?

Yes. As an artist, you are also entitled to further and separate protections for your work in the form of "moral rights," covered by the Berne Convention and the Visual Artists Rights Act (VARA).

Whereas the American copyright laws protecting artists are based on an economic concept, the legal systems in certain other countries also use a different conceptual framework, one based on the notion that works of creative expression deserve protections based on the fact that they are extensions of the artist's personality. Under such a system, for example, purchasers of a painting aren't free to do anything they want with the painting, even thought they own it. For example, they cannot mutilate the painting or display it in a manner that would be offensive to the painter. This supplementary system for protecting artists is known as the doctrine of the droit moral, or moral rights of the artist. The Berne Convention, an international agreement for protecting moral rights, agreed to by seventy-nine countries, was joined by the United States in 1989. It assures artists of certain personal rights in their artworks, even after the works have been sold or the copyright transferred. These rights are:

- The right to prevent modification, distortion, or mutilation of their artworks that would harm the artists' reputation or honor

- The right of artists to insist that their name be affixed to their work and to prevent use of their name on artworks that they did not create

- The right of artists to determine all aspects of public presentation of their artworks

- The right of artists to withdraw, destroy, or disavow any work if it is changed or no longer represents their views

The Visual Arts Rights Act

Enacted in 1990, the Visual Arts Rights Act represents the implementation into United States law of the first two Berne Convention protections: those of attribution and mutilation. VARA protects visual arts in one-of-a-kind works such as paintings, photographs, drawings, and sculptures in single or limited editions of 200 or less. Many types of artwork are excluded, such as promotional art, packaging, maps, posters, and technical drawings, to name a few. The rights under VARA are:

- **Your work may not be changed, altered, or mutilated**. For instance, nobody can cut your painting into sections and sell those sections.

- **Your work will be properly attributed to you and your name may not be used on any work that is not yours**. For instance, you can insist that your name appear on all work you create. But your name may not be placed on someone else's work.

- **You have the right to determine how your work will be displayed in public**. For instance, you have the final "okay" to any display of your work, including how it will look on a publisher's home page—how it is cropped for instance, or how it is presented in a gallery.

- **You have the right to destroy or disavow a work if it is changed**. For instance, you may disavow a computer illustration you created if your client changed elements in it such as the color or arrangements of the objects.

While VARA may be a step in furthering the rights of the artist, there are, to date, conflicting and sometimes more comprehensive protections for artists found in individual state laws. And the droit moral of the artist is still not as inclusive under VARA as under the Berne Convention. Under both doctrines, however, it is incumbent on the artist to prove that his or her reputation in the marketplace was substantially damaged by the alleged infringement.

What Is Not Protected by Copyright Law?

There are certain things that are not protected by copyright law, regardless of whether or not they are fixed in a tangible form. They are: any idea, procedure, process, system, method of operation, concept, principle, or discovery, and many lists of things such as the listings of

On The Other Hand...

Copyright protection is not extended under the Copyright Act to works of the U.S. government. A work of the U.S. government may, therefore, be reproduced and distributed without infringement liability under U.S. copyright laws. For instance, nice stock video is available from NASA. All it costs is the price of duplication. As for government forms or documents, I wonder the extent to which an artist might wish to use such items in an original artwork. I leave it to you to imagine. (Material published by state government is almost always protected by copyright.) ⤙

names, addresses, and phone numbers in the white pages of a phone book and many lists found in online databases. But be careful. If a list has been compiled using a unique methodology, or if the list is designed to look unique, it may be copyrighted.

Warning: Work Made for Hire Doesn't Belong to Its Creator

This is important. You do not own your original artwork or the copyright to it when you produce "work made for hire" (sometimes called "work for hire"). There are only two ways in which work can be work made for hire, and they're mutually exclusive. But if either applies, the work is work made for hire, and the copyright in the artwork you create for your employer belongs to your employer, not you. In fact, the copyright law considers the employer to be the "author"—which means creator—of the work.

- **You, the creator of the work, are an employee of a firm or person, and you produce the artwork as part of your job**. In general, it's easy to tell who's an employee and who isn't, but sometimes the analysis gets tricky. If you're on the payroll, and you work in the boss's offices or plant, and your supervisor can tell you how to do your job, and your job description includes the creation of artwork, then the work is work made for hire.

- **You, the creator of the work, are freelance, an independent contractor, but your client has come to you with an assignment for the work, and you and your client both sign a contract that states that your work is "made for hire," or "for hire," or has words to that effect.** It does not matter that you did the work in your own office or that you pay your own taxes and health benefits. If you have a written contract or sign a purchase order that's also signed by your client and that has words to the effect that your work is "for hire," then your client owns everything, and you're not considered the author/creator of the work.

Aside from the fact that you have nothing more to say about the way the work is used, you also lose another right, which may or may not be important to you. The Copyright Act allows the creator of work who originally owned the copyright to it (in other words, everyone who doesn't create work made for hire) to recapture it from anyone to whom it's been licensed during a five-year period that starts 35 years after the license takes effect. The creator of work made for hire doesn't have that right.

FOR WHAT IT's WORTH...

Books

Intellectual Property and the National Information Infrastructure: Report of the Working Group on Intellectual Property Rights
The Commissioner of Patents and Trademarks
U.S. Patent and Trademark Office
Box 4
Washington, DC 20231
This document contains the Working Group's efforts to deal with copyrights in the digital era. It contains an overview of the basic issues that Washington is grappling with and will give artists a flavor of the "official" government view.

Graphic Artists Guild Handbook: Pricing & Ethical Guidelines, 8th Edition
Direct Mail Distribution
Graphic Artists Guild
11 W. 20th Street
New York, NY 10011-3704
Phone: 212/463-7730
The first book an artist should purchase for information about copyrights, contracts, and pricing guidelines. The bible on these subjects, it is revised whenever industry standards change.

Copyright Law of the United States of America
Circular 92
United States Copyright Office
The Library of Congress
Phone: 202 512-1800
A nice government document. The law, chapter and verse. Not a great read, but a valuable reference for the professional artist.

Copyright Basics
United States Copyright Office
The Library of Congress
Phone: 202/512-1800

Also published by the Copyright Office, which publishes a collection of circulars on specific copyright topics. There's a catalog of circulars and other publications, many of which are of interest to visual artists.

Online

Topic 12 in the Byline Conference—ASJA Contract Watch
@well.com.
This interesting conference is for nonfiction writers, but many of the issues are parallel to those encountered by artists, especially relating to copyrights and contracts. A good resource with names of companies that have hidden work-for-hire clauses in their contracts.

hannah_klein@hud.gov
This is the government e-mail address for requesting information on copyrights (20 pages).

chapter three

WHEN COPYING IS OK

Fair Use and Other Exceptions

There are two sorts of circumstances where copying is OK. The first involves things that either lack or have lost copyright protection, such as creations in the public domain, ideas, and facts. The second involves things that are covered by copyright, but for which some instances of copying are allowable because of the Copyright Act's "fair use" exception. In this chapter I will define and explain both of these areas.

Where Copyright Protection Does Not Apply: Works That You May Copy and Use in Your Own Work

Here are the five areas where copyright protection does not apply:

- **Creations in the public domain.** Work in the public domain isn't protected by copyright. Anyone who wants to may use it freely, without asking for permission or paying a license fee. And the world is full of public-domain material. But sometimes it's not so easy to figure out just what is in the public domain. Most public-domain material got there because it's old.

There's a little complication you must be aware of when you're trying to decide whether a given work is in the public domain: two different copyright acts may apply! The first, usually called the 1909 Act, covers material created before January 1, 1978. That's when the second, called the 1976 Act because that's when it was enacted, took over.

Under the 1909 Act, the creator could obtain copyright protection for a first term of 28 years after publication and could then renew the copyright for a second 28-year term. So if the second term expired before the 1976 Act took effect, the work is in the public domain. That means that anything published first in this country before January 1, 1922, is in the public domain.

The 1976 Act sets up two categories for the length of copyright. For works that were created under the 1909 Act and that were either in their first 28-year term of copyright on January 1, 1978, or had been properly renewed and were in their second term then, the 1976 Act extends the copyright to a maximum total of 75 years from publication. So if you know a work was published more than 75 years ago, you can pretty well be sure that it's public-domain material.

For work created on or after January 1, 1978, the duration of copyright, as I said above, is the life of the author plus 50 years (or 75 or 100 years for anonymous, pseudonymous, or work-made-for-hire works). It'll be a while before anything created recently will fall into the public domain because its copyright term has expired.

- **Ideas.** Copyright protects expression of ideas, not ideas. For instance: the idea of people having a picnic on the grass is not copyrightable. Your specific execution of this idea—in which you turn your idea into something in fixed and tangible form—is copyrightable.

- **Facts**. While facts are not copyrightable, certain arrangements or interpretations of fact may be copyrighted. For instance, a list of names compiled in the white pages of the phone book is not copyrightable. But if the names were compiled using a specific formula or proprietary system of arrangement, then the names could be copyrighted.

- **Tiny parts of existing images**. Referred to as the de minimis doctrine, this allows for the copying of very small or insignificant portions of existing works. Now, on the face of it, this would seem to be the "out" you need to use just a tiny portion of a scanned image, for instance, in a photomontage. But the de minimis doctrine is not as clear as it seems. What if the small portion of the image you copy is the very essence of the copied work? Then a court might reasonably find that you have copied too much. Be very cautious when you decide that your copy is okay because it falls under de minimis standards. When in doubt, call an attorney before you use the copy.

ON THE OTHER HAND...

How much of someone else's copyrighted image did you use? Just a teeny bit. Hey, nobody's perfect. Just the leaves. From the trees. No problem. I mean, leaves are leaves, right? Fair use: so I cut up the magazine and used tiny pieces of their photos. Scanned in an ear. A finger. An eyeball. Standard body parts. And I filtered the hell out of them. You can hardly tell they're human. You certainly can't tell which human they came from. That's not infringement. Is it? And even if it is, how are they going to monitor every one-person design studio, every multigazillion dollar advertising agency, every little in-house newsletter, every account executive who scans a picture into his presentation graphics, every do-it-yourself entrepreneur with a photo-manipulation program. I mean, how? So if no police force in the world could monitor all these billions of images, why bother with copyright law? I mean. They're not going to make a test case out of my little infringements, right?

Probably not. But consider this scenario: you scan a photograph from a magazine. A bunch of flowers. You use photo-manipulation software to flop the image. But you can still tell it's the original bunch of flowers. So you edit out some of the flowers and add some leaves. It looks the same, but, you feel, it is substantially altered. You use your new image on a brochure cover for your Billion Dollar Client. The original photographer and her publisher, the magazine, sue Mr. Deep Pockets at your Billion Dollar Client, naming you as a codefendant. (See Chapter 12 for just such a "real life" infringement case.)

Or consider this example: you scan a magazine photo of a horse rearing up on its back legs. You filter it quite literally to bits. Place it in another composition, a landscape you created in a paint program. You can tell it is a horse, but you figure it's a pretty generic pose and that, because of this, nobody would ever be able to prove you copied that particular horse. You use your new image on a brochure cover for your Billion Dollar Client. But someone saw you do the scan. He turns you in. The original photographer and her publisher, the magazine, sue Mr. Deep Pockets at your Billion Dollar Client, naming you, too, as an infringer. In this situation your filtering of the image and the generic nature of the pose might create an image that a court could not say, for sure, was the scanned image. But. Someone saw you do it and turned you in. If there is a witness against you who testifies in court on these facts the judge will hold your copy to be an infringement.

- **Images that merge a concept with an execution**. This exception to copyright protection is called the merger doctrine. It is in effect where a concept and its execution are inextricably merged. For instance, two-point perspective, as a drawing technique, is a concept that will be expressed the same no matter who executes it. The execution will always have a horizon line with two vanishing points, and objects in the front will converge on the vanishing points at the horizon line. Thus the concept is said to be "merged" with the execution, and no one can copyright any form of the execution of two-point perspective, even allowing for executions in different media.

Another example is the concept of rendering a sphere on a flat surface. When an artist draws, paints, or otherwise executes the two-dimensional illusion of the three-dimensional object (in this case a sphere), she employs certain artistic conventions or concepts. She first draws a circle. She indicates a "hot spot" somewhere on the face of the circle. There is always a shaded area that radiates out from the hot spot. And there is always a bright edge at the outermost point of the circle. The use of these drawing techniques creates the illusion of a three-dimensional sphere. Any artist who wishes to create this illusion will need to use the same drawing "concepts." Without using these concepts, the execution will not look like a sphere. The concepts are merged with the execution. But you cannot copyright this technique. It is available to any artist. And, in fact, any artist who desires to render a sphere will have to use the identical concepts.

Okay. Explain Fair Use

Although the purpose of the copyright statutes is to encourage creativity by defining and protecting copyrights, there are certain times when other rights must override the rights of the artist. Generally these "fair use" exceptions were intended to protect freedom of speech (for example, by allowing book critics to quote from the book they are discussing) or to promote some sort of public benefit such as education.

Here, for the record, is the statutory language about fair use found in Section 107 of the Copyright Act (don't glaze over; read it the way you'd analyze a scene before drawing it—look at all the different elements in it):

> *Notwithstanding the provisions of section 106 and 106A, the fair use of a copyrighted work, including such use by reproduction in copies or phonorecords or by any other means specified by that section, for purposes such as criticism, comment, news reporting, teaching (including multiple copies for classroom use), scholarship, or research, is not an infringement of copyright. In determining whether the use made of a work in any particular case is a fair use the factors to be considered shall include—*
>
> 1. *the purpose and character of the use, including whether such use is of a commercial nature or is for nonprofit educational purposes;*
>
> 2. *the nature of the copyrighted work;*
>
> 3. *the amount and substantiality of the portion used in relation to the copyrighted work as a whole; and*
>
> 4. *the effect of the use upon the potential market for or value of the copyrighted work.*

When a copyright infringement case goes before a judge, and the defendant claims her image comes under the fair use exemption, the allegedly infringing image is evaluated through the lens of the stated purposes and all four factors listed above in the statute.

Using these four factors to determine whether or not a usage falls under fair use is by no means a cut-and-dried process, particularly because the language of the law itself does not make it clear just how to weigh the four factors. Courts apply them in different ways, because no two cases are identical. That means anyone who relies on fair use faces a real risk that it won't work. It can be useful, in the right circumstances, but you have to look at all the facts, and know something about how courts have used those facts, before you can feel secure. There may be many mitigating circumstances for the copying. Or there may be none. Or there may be conflicting aspects of a case, as when one of the four factors *mitigates* the usage, two factors weigh in strongly against the copying, and the last one is too *ambiguous* to decide. The answer will always depend on an objective analysis, not wishful thinking.

Let's start by looking at the purposes described in the introductory paragraph, purposes "such as criticism, comment, news reporting, teaching, scholarship, or research." A lawyer would read that list to mean that not only the purposes actually named, but others like them, would support a judge's decision that a use was fair use. The common thread among these uses is that the material claimed for fair use is what the would-be fair user is writing or drawing about. It's necessary— or at least important—*to illustrate or illuminate or to support the work in which it's being used.*

Now let's look in more detail at how the four determining factors listed above might be considered in individual cases of alleged infringement:

1. *The purpose and character of the use, including whether such use is of a commercial nature or is for nonprofit educational purposes;*

   The key word here is commercial. If someone used someone else's copyrighted image in a corporation's annual report, that person will have a more difficult time claiming a fair use exception than someone who used the same image in a free classroom reader.

2. *The nature of the copyrighted work;*

   According to the White Paper, the courts have tended to be more permissive toward copying of factual works than of works of fiction, and more permissive toward copying of published works than of unpublished works. An example of how the nature of a copyrighted work would be examined by a court could go like this: An image might be very generic as in the case of a photograph of the view of San Francisco from the 25th floor of a downtown building, facing north. Could a judge, acting as a reasonable observer, see that this photo was taken by a particular photographer? Could a judge determine that this photo was copied by just looking at it? Or decide, more probably than not, that the photo was not one taken by another photographer from, perhaps, the building next door?

3. *The amount and substantiality of the portion used in relation to the copyrighted work as a whole;*

The more of a copyrighted work you've lifted, the lower your chance of claiming a fair use exception. But the issue is not just one of quantity: as the White Paper put it, based on court decisions, "the taking of even a small amount—if it is considered the 'heart' of the work—can lead to a finding of infringement." (White Paper, p. 78).

4. *The effect of the use upon the potential market for or value of the copyrighted work.*

This is often the most important of the four factors. If your use of someone's copyrighted work has cut into that person's ability to earn money from that work, you almost certainly won't be able to establish fair use. For instance: let's say an artist created a sculpture from another artist's photograph. The derivative sculpture sells for a lot of money. It may not have hurt the market for sales of the photograph; in fact, it may have increased the market for the photograph. But it severely hurt the photographer's chances of licensing sculpture rights to any other sculptor. And that's enough to defeat a claim of fair use by the infringing sculptor. For just such a case, see Chapter 13.

Always Be Careful with Fair Use

Because what constitutes a fair use exception is a murky area of the copyright law, this is not an area where you want to take any chances. The point is this: You do not want to be in court—period. Maybe you might eventually be able to convince the judge that your use is fair use. But right now your client is steaming. Your reputation is shot. Your creative energy is being drained. It does not matter whether or not the copyright laws are crystal clear. Or whether they are fair. Or whether you are right. What matters is that litigation is a drain of money and energy that you do not need as an artist. If you want to chance it (and I don't advise that you do), that's your business. But don't whine if you get caught.

I had hoped to be able to make a nice neat list of examples where fair use is okay and examples of where it is not okay. But the list will, of necessity, be anything but comprehensive, because a court has to review each case of fair use individually, on its merits.

That said, the fair use exemption is more likely to apply when the copy:

- Is used for nonprofit educational purposes

- Is a parody of another work

- Is used for critical purposes such as in a newspaper review of a work of art

- Is used in a work of scholarship

- Is the very subject of something you're commenting on in your work

- Is strictly for your own personal use and does not affect the income of the original creator

- Does not contain the very "essence" of the original image

On the other hand, the fair use exemption would probably not apply in cases where your copy:

• Was used in a parody of the original that did not refer to the original in broad enough terms to be understood by the court

• Was used in an advertisement or commercial, or in promotional copy

• Was a complete copy of the work, or used the key elements of the work, rather than being a copy of a small portion of the work

Fair use defies unambiguous descriptions. With this in mind, I provide the following guideline that may keep you out of the netherworlds of infringement:

• When you are about to make a copy, A Strident, Annoying Bell Should Go Off in Your Head. You should heed this as a warning that you need to think clearly—and objectively—about what you are about to copy. Put yourself in the place of the person whose work you want to copy; how would she feel about what you want to do?

• Never *assume* your use falls under the fair use exemption. Never talk yourself into the fair use excuse. Do not rationalize your usage. When in doubt about copying part or all of another person's image, call for help. Get the advice of a copyright attorney (not the friendly artist in the live-work space next door), *before* you use someone else's work in your work.

ON THE OTHER HAND...

Too many artists cop to fair use. But I say, watch it, Buster! It may be fractious to say, "Hey, dream up your own images. Leave my images alone." So be it. You do not need to copy someone else's image, even to use as leavening for your own creative work. Use it for inspiration. That's ok. That's been going on for centuries. But to scan and manipulate what belongs to someone else? Not good for your karma. ☛

- When an attorney advises you to seek permission to copy someone's image, contact the person directly to ask for permission. Remember: you will need to obtain written permission before you may use the copy.

Is It Fair Use or Just Laziness?

Before you copy anyone else's art, you should consider your own motives. The artist's proud tradition of "rule breaking," at least in contemporary nineteenth- and twentieth-century art, has also contained within it a stubborn tradition of individualism. Artists struggled, with a truculent tenacity, to be utterly and completely different from anyone or anything that came before them. The Impressionists daubed at the formalism of the Academy. The Fauves upped the ante. The Action Painters threw paint all over the place. And so on. What feels different in this digital era is that artists are now appropriating elements of other artists' images, altering them digitally, and presenting the results as genuine and sincere creative explorations. But I fear they are doing this just because it is easy to do so. As image-makers, these artists create nothing but a pastiche of the minds of other creators. This copying, this risky gray area of copyrights and fair use, is only a fad. Once artists get back to true individualism, wherein they create their own unique visual statements, then there will not be so much focus on copyrights on the Net. When artists rediscover the path of rule-breaking, they will also be too proud to even consider using anyone else's images in their own creations.

FOR WHAT IT's WORTH...

Books

Multimedia Law Handbook
By J. Dianne Brinson and Mark F. Radcliffe
Ladera Press
3130 Alpine Road, Suite 200-9002
Menlo Park, CA 94025
ISBN 0-96391-0-7

A very detailed look at multimedia law. Well-written and understandable with extensive exploration of fair use situations. Also includes useful form contracts.

The Writer's Legal Companion
By Brad Bunnin and Peter Beren
Addison-Wesley Publishing Company
One Jacob Way
Reading, MA 01867
ISBN 0-201-14409-3

About the clearest and most practical discussion of copyright around, without legalisms. Good for all creators, not just writers. Filled-in forms and models for releases and permissions.

Multimedia Law for Artists: A Handbook Supplementing the Multimedia Seminar
By California Lawyers for the Arts
To obtain a copy call:
San Francisco Office: 415/775-7200
Oakland Office: 510/444-6351
Los Angeles Office: 310/395-8893

Articles and information compiled by California Lawyers for the Arts for one of their many valuable seminar sessions. A good reference.

Legal Guide for the Visual Artist
By Tad Crawford
Allworth Press
10 E. 23rd Street #400
New York, NY 10010
212/777-8395
ISBN 0-8015-4471-8

Tad Crawford writes about legal issues for artists and graphic designers. This book is a must for anyone in the business. So is his regular monthly column in Communication Arts magazine.

The Copyright Handbook: How to Protect and Use Written Works
By Stephen Fishman
Nolo Press
950 Parker Street
Berkeley, CA 94710-9867
ISBN 0-87337-241-7

This book is for writers, but it is also an excellent resource for artists. The information is very detailed but presented in a conversational manner. Copyright forms are in the back.

chapter four

GETTING PERMISSION TO USE COPYRIGHTED MATERIALS

Now That You Know When to Get Permission, Here's How

Well, of course, the previous chapter clarified, beyond a shadow of doubt, when you need to obtain permission to use works created by other artists in your own work. Sure it did. But remember: when in doubt, call an attorney. Many times you will be advised to seek permission to copy a work or portion of a work. In these cases you will need to do two things:

• Track down the creator of the work

• Obtain permission to use the work

Here is an example of a situation that requires permissions, including methods of tracking down the copyright holders and a sample permission letter.

You Are Writing a Book on Copyrights for Artists on the Electronic Superhighway

For this example, I draw from my own experience writing this book. As you can see, I use visual examples and quoted excerpts to support the text. I talked it over with my publisher. In order to determine if we needed permission to use the works, we asked ourselves the following questions:

- Is the image in the public domain?

  Most of the images I proposed to use are in the public domain. For such images, there was no need to go any further: copying them is fine. But for images that are not in the public domain, we needed to think about whether we could claim a fair use exception if we used them. So we asked ourselves:

- Are we showing them for purposes covered by the fair use exception, such as criticism, comment, or teaching?

  Yes.

- Are we using them in a nonprofit or a commercial context?

  The fact that we will market the book to a wide audience and the fact that it will be priced so as to turn a profit, for my publisher and for me, would be a negative factor in claiming a fair use exception for copying the images.

- Will the use of any of these images that are subject to copyright adversely affect the market for the artist's work?

  No, I do not believe so.

- Does any other corporation, museum, or artist's family estate own the copyrights or the right of access to any of these apparently public-domain images?

There was just enough doubt in our minds about fair use to make us seek permission to use all of the images included in this text. (We also sought permission for all of the excerpted quotes.) Nor could we assume that, just because some of the original images were quite old, they were in the public domain, because the reproductions of the original works may well have been protected by copyright. We needed to find out whether any corporation, museum, or artist's family still held copyrights to any of these images. We were uncertain on this point. It could have been possible that the Louvre, for instance owned the copyrights to the photographs of *The Balcony* by Manet that appeared in the book we were using as a source. So the next thing I had to do was to track down the potential owners of the rights and to obtain reproducible copies of the image.

How to Track Down an Image or Excerpted Quotation

Here are several ways to find out who owns the copyrights to an image or quotation. Once you determine who this is, you can contact the owner about getting written permission or licensing the rights to your particular usage. When you seek this approval you may also be able to find out about getting a transparency, continuous-tone black-and-white photograph, or digital file to use in your reproduction of the image. This list isn't comprehensive, and you may have to do some real detective work, so be prepared to spend some time and energy.

- If you want to copy an image or quote that is published in a book or magazine, contact the publisher. Addresses and sometimes phone numbers are found beneath the copyright announcement(s) in the front matter of a book or on the masthead of a magazine. If a book publisher's address does not appear in the book, try *Literary Market Place* or *Gale Directory of Publications*. When you call a publisher you should ask for the permissions department.

- If you want to copy a piece of art in the public domain, but all you can find are pictures in books, you may contact the book publisher where you find the image reproduced. Or you can contact the museum or institution that houses the work. If, for instance, you see a caption under a painting that says the work is at the Chicago Institute of Art, then call the public relations office there.

- If you are too busy to track down the origins of images you can hire a permissions specialist. They are listed in the *Literary Market Place* under permissions. These are freelance individuals who work by the project. They charge about $15 to $30 per hour.

- If a publisher has gone out of business, you can contact the Copyright Office to conduct a search. They charge $20 an hour. Phone: 202/707-6850 and ask for the Reference and Bibliography Section. Takes one or two months.

- If you are still having trouble tracking down a copyright owner, you can hire a professional copyright search firm. These firms have many people and resources at their fingertips. They can sometimes work faster than the freelancer. They work fast, but cost a lot, with fees ranging from $100 to $300 per search. Takes two to ten days. A list of copyright search firms is in Appendix C of this book.

- If you are poor and intrepid, you can search the Copyright Office records yourself. Call 800/334-2564 for information. The information is also available on the Internet at: locis.loc.gov. The password is "Copyright Information."

- If you want to scan an image from a photographer's or illustrator's own printed promotional piece, call the phone number listed on the piece.

- If you want to obtain a license to use a film clip or cartoon clip, call the public relations department of the production company listed in the credits.

- If you want to use music in your multimedia extravaganza, and you haven't commissioned a new work and hired musicians to record it (with valid contracts for everybody), then you must obtain music clearances. The music business has its own Copyright Police, and they're terrible when provoked. You can use a clearance agency such as the Harry Fox Agency, 110 East 59th Street, New York, NY 10022, phone 212/751-1930, to provide them.

Use Fees and Licensing

In some cases you can obtain permission to copy something without payment of a use fee. In other cases, you will be required to pay for the license to copy. Always be prepared to negotiate for usage fees unless you are a nonprofit, educational institution. Do not expect to avoid such fees just because you feel the original creator will be flattered you are using the work. After all, he or she is trying to make a living off such licenses. Supporting your fellow creators is just good business.

Sample Permission Letter

There are several forms of permission letter, which vary depending on the usage you seek. Note that I indicated Page 1 of 2 on the first page and Page 2 of 2 on the second. This is to inform the recipient about the length of the document in case pages are separated. Here is the permission letter I used for works from the Louvre.

28 June 1995   Page 1 of 2

Permissions Department
Service Photographique
Réunion des Musées Nationeaux
89 Avenue Victor Hugo
75116 Paris, France

I am writing to obtain permission to use the following images from the Louvre:

1) *The Balcony* by Manet, 1868.

2) *Madame Recamier* by Jacques-Louis David, 1800.

I am also requesting color transparencies or 35mm slides for use in reproduction of these images.

I wish to use these materials in the forthcoming book to be published by Peachpit Press in June of 1996:

Electronic Highway Robbery: An artist's guide to copyrights in the digital era

By Mary E. Carter

Approximate number of pages: 200

I am requesting nonexclusive world rights to use this material as part of my work in all languages and for all editions and future revisions.

Description:

Permission is requested to use the same material in all current and future versions and editions of the book in all forms and media and in related supplementary and promotional materials. We also request the right to grant the material to nonprofit institutions providing works for print or hearing-disabled students, when included in this work as a whole. Full credit will be given to the source. A release form appears below, along with space for indicating the credit line desired.

Page 2 of 2

The materials will be accompanied on publication by the following credit lines (please specify):

_____

_____

_____

If you wish these materials to be accompanied on publication by a copyright notice, please specify the form here:

_____

_____

Other conditions, if any:

_____

_____

_____

If you do not control these rights in their entirety, please specify here any additional source from whom permission must be obtained:

_____

_____

_____

Thank you for your prompt consideration of this request. A duplicate copy of this letter is enclosed for your convenience.

Very truly yours,

Mary E. Carter

The above request is approved and permission granted, subject to the conditions noted above.

Approved by: _____

Title: _____

Date: _____

Keeping Track of Permissions

Make a numbered list of all of the works for which you need permissions. The list should include the name of the work, how you are using it, the name of the copyright holder, and a place to check off when you sent the letter and when you received the reply. Place a copy of each individual permission letter in a file folder. Then mark your calendar one month from the date of the last permission letter you sent. Your list should look something like this:

	Permission Letter Sent	**Permission Rec'd**
1	Harry N. Abrams	artworks
2	Service Photographique	artworks
3	Little, Brown	artworks
4	The WELL	quote
5	Harry N. Abrams	Livingstone quote
6	Alfred Knopf	Negroponte quote
7	Barlow	Wired quote
9	Loomponics	Super Hacker quote
10	Bruce Sterling	eff quote (e-mail)
12	Dyson	Various quotes
13	Harper Collins	Barbour quote
14	PC Magazine	Zelnick quote
15	Harper Collins	Branscomb quote
16	Stecher Jag & Prutzman	Rogers v. Koons pix
17	Tony Stone Images	TS v. Arscott
18	FPG International	FPG v. Newsday
19	Joe Viesti	FPG v. Newsday
20	Corel	TS v. Arscott
21	Harry N. Abrams	Helga
22	Newsday	Newsday infringement

Then What?

Once you have mailed your permission letters, in duplicate, all you have to do is wait. And wait. And wait. Actually, in the case of permissions for this book, I received the first few permissions back in just a few days. But there were the exceptions. That's why you marked your calendar one month from the date of the last permission letter you mailed. If you have not received responses in one month, start tracking them down. The best and quickest way is to call. The phone bills will be worth the effort, and you can usually light a fire under someone, diplomatically, over the phone.

Once you have received your signed permissions, make copies of them. Place the originals in your file alongside your other important papers. Give the copies to your publisher, art gallery owner, or client for their records. That's all there is to it. Happy hunting!

Late Breaking News on the Permissions Front!

Just as this book was in the editing stage, exciting news appeared. Now it is possible to obtain some types of permissions online. If you require permission for copying materials for an educational pack or other copying for private usage, you might want to try CCC (Copyright Clearance Center) Online. Operating around the clock, CCC Online lets you search more than 1.7 million titles. Then you can determine usage fees, file electronically for permission to copy, and set up payment, all online. But CCC does not grant permissions to reprint materials in advertising, dissertations, or books. For these, you must still apply for permission in writing to the publisher of the work.

Here's the URL for Web access: http://www.directory.net/copyright/ For more information, call CCC at 508/750-8400.

FOR WHAT IT'S WORTH...

Copyright Search Firm

Government Liaison Services, Inc.
3030 Clarendon Boulevard
Arlington, VA 22201
800/642-6564

I have used the services of this firm and found it to be prompt and very helpful. Other copyright search firms are located in Arlington and Alexandria, VA, in Washington, DC, and in New York.

chapter five

HEY, THAT'S MY IMAGE!

Art Theft Was Never Easier

The hardest part about copyrights on the electronic superhighway is finding out if someone has copied your images. Copyright enforcement is the biggest problem. In this chapter I will review some of the many ways an artist can become a victim of electronic highway robbery. And I will show you how to take control of your copyrights if or when you discover you have been infringed.

On the electronic superhighway you have very little control over your images. They can be copied anywhere, by anyone. Copied digital images are clean, clear, accessible, and commercially viable as products. And they can move very swiftly away from their original creators.

On the World Wide Web, a person surfing from site to site can download any on-screen image with just a few clicks of a mouse button.

But the World Wide Web is not the only medium containing graphic images. Others include digital documents such as electronically produced newsletters, electronic faxes-on-demand, and even workgroup publications. While some portable-document software has read-only protection so that copies cannot be made of the images contained in those documents, the protection can be gotten around with certain screen-capture software. While the quality of images pirated via screen-capture software may limit their use, tools do exist to convert bit-mapped images such as screen captures into editable vector images. If your work is very graphic, with clearly delineated areas of flat color, for instance, such conversion programs can make it easy for your work to be copied. In the hands of the unscrupulous, this kind of software can become a tool for copyright infringement.

ON THE OTHER HAND...

Commercial videotapes throw the FBI warning in your face (before the commercials for coming attractions). It makes me wonder. Shouldn't scanners and screen-capture software come with a warning label: "Capturing a copyrighted image is illegal and may subject you to the penalties of law"?

Even if you don't put your images on the Web or in a portable document format, the fact that your art is in digital electronic format still increases the opportunities for someone to steal it. Let's say you put your portfolio on a CD-ROM. If someone downloads one of the images in the portfolio and puts it on the net, it's out of your control. Similarly, if your art appears in print in a magazine or a piece of advertising, anyone with a scanner can digitize it, then use one of many powerful image-manipulation tools on the market to remove the underlying dot pattern and produce a perfectly viable digital graphic file.

Off They Go into the Wild Blue Yonder

No matter what the form of digital conveyance, copies of your images are capable of traveling at light speed, to distances unimaginable until now. If it appears on a monitor and moves through the ether, it can be used or misused by anyone with the right technology. Images can be downloaded or copied, one way or another, and new digital files can be made. Work can even be altered and the resulting new digital images can be used to make printing plates, to make printed or taped products—from books to posters to films—that can be sold at a profit. Before you know it, your potential to generate income from your trade has been diminished.

With the technology in place to move digital images to the ends of the earth and to copy commercially viable products from pirated images, the artist faces the double whammy of being ripped off by someone very far away and of being ripped off very well indeed.

So. What Are You Going to Do about It?

The very first thing you need to do is to determine if the copy was used in a way that infringes your copyrights. Do not confuse mere copying with actual infringement.

If you discover that your artwork has been copied without your permission, call an attorney who specializes in copyright law. To find one, you can scan the Yellow Pages where attorneys are listed by their specialties. Or you can ask a colleague to recommend someone. Or call your local professional arts organization, such as the Society of Illustrators, the Graphic Artists Guild, or the American Institute of Graphic Artists and ask for referrals. Or call your local legal/arts advocacy group such as your state chapter of Lawyers for the Arts. Ask them for advice. The arts lawyers groups generally provide some free advice. And experienced copyright attorneys are worth the investment for the cost of an initial consultation—anywhere from $100–$400 per hour. Many lawyers will listen to your story—told briefly and without a lot of editorializing, please—without charge, to see if they're really equipped to help you. You will need professional insight into your particular case. Since your case is unique, it is a good idea to seek this advice before you decide how to proceed. An hour's worth of professional consultation can arm you with the information you need to make some important decisions. To save money, first do your homework. Write down your questions. And take notes!

After you have spoken with the copyright attorney, go home. Relax. Gather your thoughts and have a heart-to-heart discussion with yourself. Just say, "Self, what's at stake here?" Then ask yourself these questions:

- Was this a case of infringement? Am I badly damaged by this act of infringement? Is this a major act of infringement? Has the person taken a whole work or just part of a work?

- Have I lost a significant amount of income due to this infringement? Is my market seriously hurt? Is my potential to create a valuable derivative work ruined because of this copy?

- Is my reputation affected by this act of infringement? Will it damage my professional relationship with my clients or an art gallery, for instance?

- Am I extremely offended by this infringement? Is this going to bug me if I don't follow up on it?

Once you have gauged the seriousness of the issue, you have several alternatives.

Send the infringer a "cease and desist" letter. Regardless of how you intend to proceed, the first step will be to send the infringer a letter that tells the infringer to stop copying. In addition, the letter can demand compensation for the copying that has occurred. Your attorney can help you write this letter or can write it for you. Don't threaten a lawsuit in this letter unless you're really prepared to pursue one. If you're lucky, the infringer will stop and agree to the requested payment, in which case you at worst will have prevented any further damage and at best been fully compensated as well. In any case, if you do intend to take matters further up the ladder of justice, you will still need to start with a cease and desist letter to put the infringer on notice. It's important to keep in mind that sending that letter does not commit you to a long and expensive legal battle later on. Since these letters frequently work, they are actually a good way to stay *out* of court. By the way, the tone of the letter may have something to do with the infringer's response. It's almost always better to write a letter that's firm but does not accuse the infringer of devil worship. Stick to the facts as you understand them, and make your demand crystal clear: "Please stop using my image in your book, and please notify me in writing that you've done so. I believe a fair permissions fee to be $500. If I have to pursue this further, the price will probably go up. I need your response by 5:00 P.M. on March 15, 1996."

Take the infringer to arts arbitration or mediation. This route is open only if you have a contract with your infringer that includes an arbitration or mediation clause, or if the infringer is willing to let the mediator help you work out a solution or to let the arbitrator decide the case. (That's the difference, by the way: mediators don't tell you what you have to do; arbitrators do.) Many professional arts organizations provide arbitration and mediation services, as do all of the arts lawyer groups. In addition to providing for arbitration or mediation, your contract must name who will function as the arbitrator or mediator should a dispute arise between you and your employer or client. While it is not required that you have an attorney in an arbitration hearing, your opponent may show up with an attorney. You may want to hire an attorney, too, even though you do not have to. In that case, even arbitration and mediation can cost a lot. And the process may be as draining as an actual court case, although it will probably not drag on for years to get "your day in court" with the arbitrator.

Take the infringer to court. If other options are not available or fail, your final option is to sue. You might arrive at a decision to sue if you determine that your financial or professional damages are very great. Going to court is the most expensive route for the individual artist. Fees for intellectual property litigators range from $125 to $400 an hour, perhaps even more in New York or Los Angeles. And a lawsuit can take months or years to resolve. Pursuing an infringer can get very expensive, even if you win. But more importantly, the costs of litigation, if it should come to that, go way beyond money. There are the mental stresses and emotional strains of preparing a legal battle. Multiply these by the number of months or years required to get your case to court. As an artist, this can be a substantial drain on your creative energy. If you and your career have taken a major "hit" then you may decide that you have to go to court. Yours may be the valuable precedent-setter that will benefit the entire arts community. And you may collect major damages for the harm caused you. But litigation is both expensive and uncertain, so be sure you know what you're getting into before you commit to it.

What happens when you win your suit? Collecting the damages you win can be as much of a problem as the original lawsuit. The loser might appeal the decision, dragging the case through yet another long court battle. Meanwhile, you might not have collected a dime. Or the loser may have no money (or may have hidden it well). Court battles are not for the impatient or the faint of heart.

Did You Know That Copyright Law Enforcement Is Optional?

Except for extremely flagrant offenses, most types of copyright infringement fall under the category of civil offense, which means that it is up to the person who has been infringed to seek justice and redress. That is not to say that great sums of money cannot be at stake.

While the typical value of a copyright infringement is probably in the range of $500 to $5,000, some copyright infringement cases can involve hundreds of thousands of dollars in damages and attorneys' fees.

But unlike traffic laws and criminal laws, copyright laws are almost never enforced by the police, despite that FBI warning on the videotapes. It is usually up to the individual copyright holder to discover infringements and to decide whether or not to go to court.

FOR WHAT IT's WORTH...

Organizations

American Institute of Graphic Arts
164 Fifth Avenue
New York, NY 10010
212/807-1990

California Lawyers for the Arts
Fort Mason Center, Building C, Room 255
San Francisco, CA 94123
415/775-7200

Graphic Artists Guild
11 W. 20th Street, 8th Floor
New York, NY 10011
212/463-7730

HOW THEY SEE IT— PARTIES TO THE COPYRIGHT DEBATE

The Technocrat, The Attorney, and The Artist Take Tea. A Fable.

In an unlikely convergence, four movers and shakers of the digital era decided to meet for tea to discuss copyrights on the electronic superhighway. They were the brilliant copyright attorney, Harriet Lawlor; the Washington D.C. Chair of the Working Group on Copyability, Harold Committeeman; the handsome and wild-eyed technology visionary, Ted Nickel; and the 1994 Gaggledorfer Fellow, well known digital artist, Etha Reale. After the introductions, the meeting came to order.

Harold, accustomed as he was to the loneliness of commanding committee meetings, tapped his spoon on the table and began: "We are here to discuss the meaning and relevance of copyright laws for artists and artworks on the Electronic Superhighway. As we all know, copyright laws make it possible for artists to exist in a reproducible world. But will the laws survive the digital era?"

Harriet Lawlor answered, "Yes indeed they will. Why, without copyright laws the artist would be afraid to put her works online for fear of it being stolen by parties of the second part."

"No. No. NO," broke in Ted Nickel, "All information wants to breathe free. And surely art is just that, just 0s and 1s, pure information, roaming the networks at the speed of light into the faces of screenmeisters all over the virtual globe."

"Au contraire, Mr. Nickel," cut in Harriet, "You gotta have laws to protect the innocent creator in the digital jungle!"

"Yes, BUT!", burst in Etha Reale, "No book of rules, no laws, will stifle nor inspire me. I am The Artist! I WILL create. Regardless. I will float my creations hither and yon. Off-line or on." She paused, frowning, "But God save the little sucker who steals my artwork on the net," she finished somewhat ungraciously.

"People. People," Harold Committeeman moderated, clanking his spoon with parliamentarian emphasis. "PEOPLE! We are all in agreement here, I believe. We want laws, laws, laws. Yet we want to be free, free, free. Is that not what we are about here today?"

The tea party had gone tepid. No sooner had discussion begun, than it had jammed to a screeching halt. The Bureaucrat, the Technocrat, the Attorney and the Artist were caught in a traffic jam of irreconcilable differences. Copyrights on the superhighway were stuck.

Meanwhile, back in the real world...

This hyperbolic little fable illustrates the cast of characters involved in determining how copyright law evolves these days. The policy makers for copyright in the digital era are: Washington DC bureaucrats and politicians, artists, technology visionaries, advertising agency art directors, hackers, and cyberspace iconoclasts. Then there are the corporate communications industries from phone companies to entertainment empires. And let's not forget the effect that the general public has on the politicians.

Each party sees the copyright issue from a different perspective, a perspective so skewed at times as to represent an entirely different world view from the other parties to the debate.

The issues? It all centers around whether or not copyright law will work on the electronic superhighway. Opinions abound. Words are flying back and forth with speed and velocity. Camps have developed. For a look at who is saying what, here are a few brief chapters which sum up the various points of view.

chapter six

HOW WASHINGTON GRAPPLES WITH IT

The Many Arms of the Octopus

As the United States government attempts to deal with the need to bring copyright law into the digital era, many powerful interests are demanding to be heard. Among those participating in the debate are numerous government agencies; the House of Representatives and the Senate; international trade organizations; the powerful and increasingly conglomerated telephone, communications, computer, and entertainment corporations; various other special interest groups; *and* general public opinion.

ON THE OTHER HAND...

Hey! What about the artists? Is anybody listening to us?... Is that an echo I hear? 🐂

The existence of so many groups with a stake in the outcome and the conflict inherent in the process itself make the going rough and can, in some cases, make the outcome look like a horse made by a committee—which, indeed, it probably will be.

In understanding where the government is headed on the issue of copyright law, it's useful to remember the purpose of copyright in the first place. In the United States, that purpose is basically an economic one. It sees the protection of intellectual properties as the prime motivator of creative output.

According to this perspective, if the government wants to see the electronic highway develop into a true

"National Information Infrastructure," it needs to make sure that the laws are strong enough to protect the owners of intellectual property rights—writers, entertainment conglomerates,and so on—so that they will want to use this new means of distribution.

To quote from the White Paper (*Intellectual Property and the National Information Infrastructure*):

> *Owners of intellectual property rights will not be willing to put their interests at risk if appropriate systems...are not in place to permit them to set and enforce terms and conditions under which their works are made available in the NII [National Information Infrastructure] environment.*

Remember that the "owners of intellectual property" referred to here are not just individual writers and artists, but also some of the largest and most powerful corporations in the world. They have the most at stake in the copyright battle, and Washington will focus on their concerns first.

I have said it before, the reason that copyright law is now under such heavy scrutiny by lawmakers hinges on three important changes in the way in which intellectual property (read artworks) can be copied and transmitted. Each has to do with technology and digital imaging:

- Digital images can travel very great distances from their originators.

- Digitally transmitted images can produce an excellent "file" that may be effectively reproduced and sold.

- Digital images are much easier to change, in dramitic ways, than hard copy.

In light of these three changes, the first item of business is simply making sure that the laws protecting copyrights on the electronic highway are enforceable. The following quote from *Intellectual Property Rights in an Age of Electronics and Information* is but the tip of the iceberg in the area of enforcement. It represents a key concern to artists who decide to put their works online:

> *A problem of identifying infringements and enforcing rights: The increased communications capacity... made possible by fiber optic technology will allow computer users to rapidly transmit incredible amounts of information... these high-speed communications media... pose enforcement problems for the intellectual property system. They allow individuals to trade vast quantities of copyrighted materials without the knowledge or permission of copyright holders.... Moreover, using computer networking technology, they can now easily and inexpensively reproduce and transmit copyrighted works.*

> *This remarkable state of affairs raises several problems for the copyright system. First, if a private citizen copies information—a film or a record for example—should this be considered an infringement of copyright?... Second, if it were decided that home copying infringed copyright, how could a ban against it be enforced? Since many people could be engaged in this kind of behavior in the privacy of their own homes, their activities would be impossible to track. (Intellectual Property Rights in an Age of Electronics and Information, p. 6)*

That Washington holds these concerns about enforcement of copyrights in the digital era is critically important to anyone who uses the Net.

Enforceability leads to two other key concerns. The first of these is protection of civil liberties, especially privacy. For example, encryption promises to be an important tool for protecting intellectual property; yet law enforcement agencies within government have generally opposed the free use of encryption, thinking encryption could be used by criminals to hide their transactions.

A second key concern is the international dimension. Not all nations observe U.S. copyright laws. In fact, some pretty big countries—China in particular—don't hold with our copyrights at all or have copyright laws on the books that are not vigorously enforced.

As Washington wrestles with such tough problems as enforcement of copyrights on the electronic highway, the relation between encryption and privacy, and various international implications, powerful lobbies are pushing to make sure that their particular interests are protected. For example, the movie industry has focused on laws preventing excessive videocassette piracy. And U.S.-based software companies, most significantly Microsoft, are concerned about blatant piracy of their products overseas. In this general mob scene, I highly doubt that we artists are the ones with the sharpest elbows.

ON THE OTHER HAND...

So where's the artist in all this? Who's going to listen to our needs? Who represents our interests in all of this? I suspect that the inarticulate and disparate requirements of our "set" have little impact on the real movers and shakers in Washington. Scant priority is given to "feelings" or aesthetic sensibilities. I have a feeling we artists will remain outside the process, a pesky fringe constituency, at best.

I'd like to close this discussion of the role of government with a different voice, that of the individual artist. Here is a quote from the OTA *Workshop on the Impact of Technology on the Creative Environment*, April 24, 1985. During that workshop the actor Theodore Bikel had this to say:

The arts are about risk taking. More often than not [they are] about endangerment. You endanger your soul each time you put some pen to paper, each time you try to interpret somebody else's words. We are about poetry. We are about the gossamer fabric of hopes, of dreams.

To summarize the government's point of view: Washington works with the inevitable push and pull of public opinion and corporate interests. It sits at the hearing table and tries to blend the often opposing views and motivations of these disparate groups. On the table are the issues of enforceability of copyrights in the digital era, the changing marketplace for intellectual property, and lack of worldwide copyright protection. Watch it on C-Span. Democracy is slow. Washington assumes that the world revolves around law and money. But artists float above the fray. Creating new realities. Fixed on their own stars.

And all the while, technology speeds frenetically onward, its proponents contemplating visions far beyond the imagination of the bureaucrats. Next we will consider copyright from that dizzying perspective.

ON THE OTHER HAND...

Heady stuff for the enclaves of law. I find it hard to believe that artists would simply never create a thing if it were not for copyright protection. I would make my art whether it were aided by the existence of copyright law or not. At great risk. Or at little risk. Hey, I've already put my artwork on the Web. Knowing full well it could be pirated. I would make art even if it were illegal to do so, comes to that. And while I need to pay the rent just as much as the next guy, the monetary component of copyright law—the preservation of my right to sell and distribute my work—is most assuredly not the principal reason I make my art. The Big Guys might be motivated by copyright law. But not the artist in her studio.

FOR WHAT IT's WORTH...

Publications

Intellectual Property Rights in an Age of Electronics and Information
Office of Technology Assessment
United States Congress
E-mail Linda Garcia at: lgarcia@ota.gov

The now-defunct Office of Technology Assessment was a research arm of the Congress. It monitored and collected vast amounts of information about technology and about its effects on society and law.

Intellectual Property Rights in an Age of Electronics and Information is a 300-page document that examines the state of technology and intellectual property as of April 1986. It includes exhaustive research about the effects of technology and communications on copyrights. It is filled with reports from various OTA Workshops. Information has been gleaned from actors, musicians, and artists, from technology experts, economists, and marketers and media moguls. While the report is somewhat dated, in that new technologies have escalated the issues, it is filled with concepts that still apply to copyrights and the creators who own them.

Intellectual Property and the National Information Infrastructure
c/o Terri A. Southwick, Attorney-Advisor
Office of Legislative and International Affairs
U.S. Patent and Trademark Office
Box 4
Washington, DC 20231

This White Paper was prepared by the Working Group on Intellectual Property Rights, made up of representatives from various agencies. The purpose of the document was to examine and analyze the intellectual property implications of the National Information Infrastructure. This 238-page document presents an overview of information obtained from the executive and legislative branches of government and from the public. To quote from the Introduction of the document: "The special intellectual property concerns and issues raised by the development and use of the NII are the subject of this Report; it does not attempt to address all existing intellectual property issues."

The White Paper sets out legal and historic background materials about copyrights. It summarizes copyright law. And it discusses how technology will impact the law. Many copyright case histories are presented and reviewed. And, lastly, the White Paper sets out to define areas of copyright law that may require change. Interestingly, there are few recommendations for changing the laws themselves. The Working Group appears to lean in the direction of technology—such as encryption, for example—to protect copyrighted material.

chapter seven

How Technocentrists Challenge It

Who Are These Guys, Anyway?

Technology visionaries, from the Media Lab at MIT, for instance, and other key pioneers on the Internet, bring a certain creative experimentalism to their view of copyright issues. For these people, the digital age moves at a much more rapid speed than it does for Washington lawmakers.

Technology visionaries view copyright law as a slow-moving dinosaur, well on its way to extinction in the incendiary new digital age. I call these folks "technocentrists." That is, they view copyright law—the whole world, for that matter—from the perspective of technology. And since technology evolves in swift incandescence, these technocentrists are most like the artist in character. Experimental. Fearless. Blundering. Excitable. Tangential. And wildly creative.

Technocentrism on the Wild Frontier

What follows here is a barrage of quotes taken from the key thinkers of the digital era. I present them here in clips and gulps, rapid-fire, in the spirit of the speakers. These are the people who live, eat, breathe, and sleep— if they do sleep—the Internet.

Copyright law is totally out of date. It is a Gutenberg artifact. Since it is a reactive process, it will probably have to break down completely before it is corrected... a painter more or less kisses a painting good-bye upon its sale. Pay-per-view would be unthinkable. On the other hand, in some places it is still perfectly legal to chop up the painting and resell it in smaller pieces, or to replicate it as a carpet or beach towel without the artist's permission.

(From *Being Digital* by Nicholas Negroponte, Professor of Media Technology at MIT and Founding Director of the Media Lab)

Perhaps those who are part of the problem will simply quarantine themselves in court, while those who are part of the solution will create a new society based, at first, on piracy and freebooting. It may well be that when the current system of intellectual property law has collapsed, as seems inevitable, that no new legal structure will arise in its place.

(From "The Economy of Ideas: A Framework for Rethinking Patents and Copyrights in the Digital Age [Everything You Know About Intellectual Property Is Wrong]," *Wired Magazine*, by John Perry Barlow, Cofounder and Executive Chair of the Electronic Frontier Foundation)

Part of my research for this book was done online at The WELL. At the suggestion of Mike Godwin, chief attorney for the Electronic Frontier Foundation, I opened a topic in the eff (Electronic Frontier Foundation) conference. I asked if there was anyone in the conference who held that copyrights would not work in the digital era. Among the responses were these comments, reprinted here with the permission of Bruce Sterling:

Topic 686 [eff]: Copyright laws online.

#16 of 19: Bruce Sterling (bruces)   Tue Apr 4 '95 (11:19)

Uhm, well, I see a basic three possible scenarios:

1. Intellectual property wins and data pirates remain a kind of pesky fringe scum (ISLANDS IN THE NET)

2. *Some entire new means of publication comes about, probably with power shifting from publishers and authors to critics, editors, and assemblers (attention economy), and*

3. *Perhaps the most interesting scenario, the information economy crashes worse than Marxism, everything gets entirely and utterly screwed up, no governmental policy of any kind is ever able to effect anything, nothing stabilizes, nothing is workable, no theory makes sense, chaos ensues and it stays that way forever (HEAVY WEATHER).*

I hope this helps *8-)

Bruce Sterling is author of *Islands in the Net, The Artificial Kid,* and *The Hacker Crackdown: Law and Disorder on the Electronic Frontier.*

Then there is this oft-quoted sentence from Stewart Brand's book *The Media Lab*:

Information wants to be free.

Strange that the very next sentence written by Brand, which reads, "Information also wants to be expensive," is never quoted along with the first. In that chapter of *The Media Lab*, Brand goes on to explore copying, copyrights, and remuneration for content creators. He focuses on digital sampling in the music industry and discusses the issues of collecting royalties and creative "leakage,"

ON THE OTHER HAND...

I like Sterling's third scenario. The anarchy and all. A kind of Jackson Pollack of the Internet. Down with draftsmanship! Forget imagery! Let's get a little action into our painting! We're gonna make something beautiful out of flinging our paints around. Who knows what might happen? But it'll be big and gorgeous and it'll change the nature of painting forever. Pollack was right. So, maybe these guys are right, too. Just fling those copyrights out. It'll be big and splashy and it'll change the nature of copyrights forever. 🐂

wherein not all copyrighted material is paid for by the end users. He carefully analyses each side of the issue: the creator's need to be paid for her work and the copyists' desire to obtain the work for nothing. And he discusses the increasing ease with which technology provides the means to copy. Copying and copyrights and their corollary, payment schemes for creators, are his focus. Brand's exploration is broad and thoughtful.

But somewhere along the line, the only trace element that remains of his chapter on information and copyrights is the phrase, "Information wants to be free." It's a shame, because the material that follows from that lead is meaty and thought provoking. But that single phrase has been taken up like a mantra by those who want an excuse to take everything that's out there in the digital universe. Everyone from hackers to high-technology groupies are tossing around that phrase. Out of context, it has an odd ring to it. More about this in Chapter 19.

And Watch Out for Those Technological Whiz Kids, the Hackers

To include hackers with technocentrists may offend some folks. But the relationship between these two groups has long been established. Founders of the Electronic Frontier Foundation defended the most famous of the hackers in the 1990 crackdown on hackers. As for the hacker view of intellectual property, one line pretty much sums it up, and it comes from the Knightmare, computer hacker and author of *Secrets of a Super Hacker*:

> *All of humanity should have the ability to access virtually any known information.*

He's not in it for the money, just for the challenge of the "hack." Some hackers even believe they are performing a variety of public service when they crack into an information system. Some hackers will go so far as to warn people that the information on their computers, which they, the hackers, have accessed, could be stolen by less scrupulous people.

What hackers represent to the artist, and to copyrights in general, is a kind of outlaw mentality and skill set. While many hackers hold themselves to be above crass theft of digital information, with a professed duty only to the art of the "hack," the skills of the hacker are not always in the hands or minds of such honest folk. The skills of the hacker, in the hands of the unscrupulous, can wreak havoc with copyrights. If artists attempt to lock their images on the Net (see a discussion of technological locks in Chapter 15) it will be hackers, or those with their skills, who will break the locks.

To Copyright or Not to Copyright? That Is the Question

In their sheer ebullience, these views are somehow attractive to this artist. The newness of the technology sparks creativity, both aesthetically and ethically. Maybe it's time for new art and new laws. Together, these technocentrists have dedicated thousands of hours of thinking to the subjects of copying and life on the Net. Quoting them here barely does them justice. But, as an artist, I am intrigued by the concept of both the free flow of all information and a loosening of copyright constraints, at least online. And, while I am tugged back and forth, I see things here that I would want law and policy makers to add to their mix.

FOR WHAT IT's WORTH...

Books and Articles

Being Digital
By Nicholas Negroponte
Alfred A. Knopf, Inc.
201 E. 50th Street
New York, NY 10022
ISBN 0-679-43919-6

A series of articles exploring the vast reaches of cyberspace. Written by one of the foremost thinkers of the digital era. Negroponte is the Founding Director of the Media Lab at MIT and Professor of Media Technology at MIT. His regular column in *Wired* pushes the outermost edges of the copyright debate and the future of mankind in the digital era.

"Copyrights and Wrongs" by Brad Bunnin
Publish, April 1990

A balanced discussion of copyright law and the new technologies. The article won an award from the Computer Press Association.

"The Economy of Ideas: A Framework for Rethinking Patents and Copyrights in the Digital Age (Everything You Know About Intellectual Property Is Wrong)," by John Perry Barlow
Wired, March 1994

This is a "must" for anyone interested in copyrights in the digital era. Barlow is Cofounder and Executive Chair of the Electronic Frontier Foundation; a retired cattle rancher; and a lyricist for the Grateful Dead.

The Hacker Crackdown
By Bruce Sterling
Bantam Books
1540 Broadway
New York, NY 10036
ISBN 0-553-56370-X

A fascinating look into the world of hackers and their defenders. Reveals the hysteria surrounding hacking, within the ranks of the general public and in the law enforcement community. Sterling is one of the leading observers of cyberspace and has written many volumes on the subject.

The Media Lab: Inventing the Future at MIT
By Stewart Brand
Viking Books
Penguin USA
375 Hudson Street
New York, NY 10014
ISBN 0-670-81442-3

An in-depth look at what's going on at MIT. Brand was founder, editor, and publisher of *The Whole Earth Catalog; he was founder of the WELL (Whole Earth 'Lectronic Link); winner of the National Book Award 1972; consultant in 1968 to Douglas Englebart's Augmented Human Intellect program at SRI; and organizer of the first Hacker's Conference.*

Secrets of a Super Hacker
By The Knightmare
Introduction by Gareth Branwyn
Loompanics Unlimited
P.O. Box 1197
Port Townsend, WA 98368
ISBN 1-55950-106-5

An excellent look into the world of the hacker. This book introduces the reader to the mind behind the hack, as well as the tools of the trade.

 "Who Owns Art in the Digital Era?" by Gene Gable
Publish, February 1994
A roundtable discussion featuring artists, computer people, lawyers, and publishers. No holds barred.

chapter eight

HOW ATTORNEYS VIEW IT

Order. Order. Order in the Court

The legal field of copyright is notorious for its complexity and intellectual challenge. In 1841, Supreme Court Justice Story described copyright law and case history as:

> ...nearer than any other class of cases...to what may be called the metaphysics of law where the distinctions are, or at least may be, very subtle and refined, and, sometimes, almost evanescent.

Maybe because of the inherent difficulty of copyright law, copyright lawyers seem to be the players in the debate who know best where their marks are. In general, copyright attorneys agree on these things:

- Copyright laws will work on the electronic super-highway with little or no change in the current statutes.

- Technology—encryption, tracking use online, and so on—will come to the aid of the artist for the protection of copyrighted images in the digital era.

At this writing, copyright attorneys are waiting for the really big test cases to arrive on the legal scene. There is a consensus among them that we are yet to hear about some of the thorniest issues around copyright in the digital era. While there are degrees of separation among leading copyright attorneys—from those who believe there will be dramatic changes in how copyrights will be handled on the Net to those who believe that any changes will be but small compass adjustments—they are generally convinced that the laws will prevail, that the precedent-setting cases will prove the strength of current copyright statutes. They also believe that technology will supply the artist with the means to enforce copyrights in the future.

In the course of researching this book I interviewed eight copyright attorneys in depth and spoke with numerous others at conferences and advocacy groups. For the attorneys, law and precedent, the Constitution, and the jury system were the accustomed props. Yet, there is a sense of anticipation among the group. Waiting for the cases of the future to play out. They all smiled confidently when I asked my leading question, "What do you say to those who hold that all information wants to be free?" The general consensus was that the laws would prevail.

chapter nine

How Art Directors Cope With It

It's Been Going on Forever

As a former advertising agency copywriter, I can attest to the daily use of a wide variety of images in comprehensive layouts. As I researched for this book, the agency art directors repeatedly asked me this question:

> *May I use images—from artists' or photographers' promotional CDs for instance, or scans from the previously published work of an artist—for use in comprehensive layouts?*

Agency art directors are very concerned about copyrights in the digital era. And it's a whole new world out there. The answer to the question is simple: Strictly speaking, no. It is an infringement of the copyrights of the photographers or illustrators whose work you scan for use in your comp. And, strictly speaking, you should pay them a licensing fee for using their image (or part of their image) in a comp.

But artists, photographers, artists' representatives, art directors, and graphic designers have mixed feelings about this kind of usage. And lest you think that the use of images in comps is just nickel and dime stuff, see Chapter 11. In the case of *Tony Stone Images v. Steven Arscott*, the plaintiff was asking for $400,000 in damages for the alleged copying of one of its images in a *mock* layout. This mock layout won a major award, the CorelDraw contest. Corel awards winners with both cash and hardware prizes. So the humble comprehensive layout ended up with a very high value. If the comp had been used *solely* to sell a concept to a client, then very likely nothing would have come of it. But entering it to win a major prize changed the picture dramatically, by subjecting the infringing use to wide publicity and by awarding it. *That* the plaintiff found impossible to accept.

How the Various Parties to the Comping/Copyright Controversy Line Up

The Reps

For artists' representatives, it is almost impossible to discover when or if an art director is using an image. Agencies produce hundreds of comps daily. If the art director has had the courtesy and professionalism to call the rep, obtaining a purchase order for every image comped into the many, sometimes hundreds, of experimental layouts can become a logistical and budgetary nightmare for art directors, reps, and artists. It's hard enough getting POs for the actual assignments when they go out.

Some artists' representatives feel it is just not worth it, financially, to pursue usage fees for comps. What can you charge for having part of your artist's promotional piece or previously produced artwork scanned into a layout? It is hard to keep track of these small usages and hard to encourage follow-through for sums of money under a hundred or so dollars.

For photographers' representatives it is quite a different story. They and the photographers they represent are very strict in the enforcement of usage fees for images used in comprehensives. They have strong professional organizations that work to educate art directors and designers about contacting them for such licensing.

Art Directors and Graphic Designers

For art directors and graphic designers this is a sticky area. "Comping" has gone on "forever." It never used to be such an issue. But now that digital files look so good, there is a new awareness of the value of the comprehensive in the sale of a layout or design to the clients. Some art directors are nervous about their past usages, afraid they might one day be dragged into court over such copying. Logistically, it is a time-consuming and paperwork-intensive job to track down each and every artist or photographer whose work might appear in the many hundreds of comps an art director produces in the course of developing just a single advertising campaign.

A Middle Path

Given the issues and varying opinions, here is a safe strategy for dealing with comps. If you are an artist, illustrator, or photographer you may want to waive your copyrights in such usages (if, indeed, you ever discover your work has been used in a comp) because you stand a chance of getting hired to do the actual job if the concept ever gets approved. It's a form of self-promotion.

If you are an agency art director or graphic designer, you should at least call the artist, photographer, or rep regarding images you want to comp. Ask them for permission to use the work. And, of course, if you want to use images from a stock photo house, *always* call and find out what the comp policy is. This way, you have done the legal thing; you have contacted the copyright owner to get a license.

The artist or photographer may very well waive her copyrights in the above-mentioned manner. But consider this, too: if you persuade the artist to waive her fee in light of the fact that, if approved, she will get to do the final work and then you do not hire her for the job when the layout is approved—for any reason whatsoever—you will have used copyright law *against* that artist. She will have gambled on getting the project assignment, waived a legitimate and legal use fee for the license to use her work in a comp, and lost.

Consciousness Raising

With the new focus on copyrights in the digital era, a lot of heads have been turned round. What was once an everyday practice is now the subject of much spirited discussion. But no matter on what side you come out, copyrights are at stake. Maybe we have the excellence of the digitally copied files to thank—or curse—for this. But the focus on copyrights in the advertising industry will only work to help the artist.

COPYRIGHT CASE HISTORIES

You have just put down the receiver of your telephone after spending half an hour with tech support and, by the grace of good technology and a friendly voice on the other end of the line, finally, you have installed Netscape. You tune in. By a simple point and click you access a web page and silently, suddenly, you are net-surfing, roaming rudderless in the World Wide Web. Where am I? You wait impatiently as a snapshot comes into view, line by line, slowly, too slowly, will this thing never down-load? And there you sit, mesmerized and tech-nologized, staring idiotically into your computer terminal, waiting for the world. It's a snapshot of a tall fellow stand-ing on the beach and next to it is some text, hyper text, with little phrases highlighted and, in a kind of friendly story, you're reading all about this guy's life. You click on one of the words and, blink, you're on another screen and some other image is meticulously, painfully slowly, unraveling and where is *this* anyway? You get bored, click another "button" and you are, maybe, in an art gallery and you read a bit, then click an artist's name and, blink, you see her images, tiny, grainy, postage stamps on your raster screen. And, hey, is this art? Am I supposed to like this? I can hardly *see* this thing! And where am I?

You peer myopically, leaning first closer, then further away from your computer screen, trying to get a real good look a the little image. It's. It's nice, I guess. I like this woman's work.

Now let's see, how do I do this thing. I think I'll download it and take a closer look. Maybe I could use that red bit there in one of my multi-media things. Click. I do it. It looks great, just the right visual punctuation to go with the Cranberries song I'm using for the background music.

You have just broken the law. All alone, sitting quietly in your studio, with no real malice aforethought, you are a common, thieving, scofflaw—worse, an ART THIEF!

chapter ten

PREPARING FOR THE CASES

Your Day in Court

In the following chapters I present three recent cases of copyright infringement. Two of the cases are settled. One is still pending. As you review the materials, I suggest that, as an exercise, you be the judge. These cases will help you to look at and really "see" images that are, or have been, in dispute. By studying these cases, both visually and in the facts presented, you can exercise your understanding of copyright law and of the copyability of images that are "out there." As you look at these cases, take into consideration fair use and the other situations where copying is okay. These are the foundations of copyright law that a judge and jury will use when reviewing these actual cases.

There are also two other interesting factors that a judge could apply when deciding if an image infringes. I call these factors the Judge's Test. They are a synthesis of questions that the attorneys posed as we discussed cases of infringement and samples of actual artworks. These three questions provide further insight when reviewing the content of images that might be in dispute.

The Judge's Test

- What is your instant gut level response to this image? Infringement? Or not?

- What does close analysis of the elements of the two images tell you? Are there strong similarities in content, structure, organization?

- Was the artist just too lazy to come up with her own image? Is this just too much a copy and not enough an original—if inspired—concept?

But First, a Review

Chapter 2 outlines the basics of copyright law. Here they are again so you can have them at your fingertips while considering the following alleged infringements. Use the law and the Judge's Test as you review the following infringement cases.

The Law

Here is an abbreviated summary of the main points of the law. These are just reminders. If you find yourself cringing as you apply them, then turn back to Chapter 2 for more detailed discussions of the concepts.

Exceptions to copyright law, that is, situations in which you are allowed to copy another person's image, include:

- Creations in the public domain. Remember that work falls into the public domain when its copyright protection expires, after many years. The rules are a little complicated, so review them if you have any doubt.

- Ideas are not protectible; expressions of ideas are.

- Facts.

- Very small portions of existing images.

- Images that merge a concept with an execution— for instance any execution of perspective.

- Fair use, including parody and editorial uses. Copying for educational or classroom use, criticism, scholarship, commentary, news reporting, and research purposes. Note that the appropriateness of a Fair Use exception depends on many things, including the purpose and character of the use, the nature of the work and the extent of the copying, and whether the copying harms the potential market for the work.

Preview of the Cases

Before I reveal the details and/or settlements of the following cases, take a look for yourself. Examine the side-by-side images and these brief descriptions of the disputed usages. Consider each case based on the law and the Judge's Test and jot down your thoughts. You may feel ambiguous about the usage. In that case, write down a few notes to compare with the actual cases presented in the next few pages. This exercise will help hone your copyright knowledge and will raise your awareness of images in "the real world."

Tony Stone Images v. Stephen Arscott

Stephen Arscott created a mock book cover, *The Real West,* which he entered in the CorelDraw 1994 World Design Contest (Figure 4 on page 221). His entry was the grand-prize winner, for which he was eligible to receive cash and computer hardware as a prize. His attorney said that Arscott did not electronically reproduce or scan the photograph, but that "He did take a photograph and reproduce it. He made a drawing in CorelDraw, but he did not do anything electronically to infringe TSI's copyright."

Tony Stone Images sued. One of the photographers they represent is Nick Vedros, the photographer of the image entitled *Potawatamie Indian* (Figure 5). According to TSI's director of photography, Sarah Stone, "The use of *Potawatamie Indian* was a blatant copyright infringement."

FPG International v. Newsday

FPG International represents the photographer James Porto. He created all of the original elements in the composite image show in Figure 6 on page 222. That is, all of the photographs came from his own stock library of photos he shot specifically for an intended purpose. FPG International has exclusive rights to license Porto's images, and *Newsday*, a newspaper with a circulation of nearly one million, used the image without permission.

Newsday, however, flopped the image and made alterations to it. And Newsday combined Porto's image with yet another image, a photo of the Dallas skyline, by another photographer, Joe Viesti. The revised image (Figure 7 on page 222) appeared on the front page of *Newsday*'s Sunday Supplement, illustrating a story about virtual reality. *Newsday* claimed the infringement was "inadvertent" because the computer illustrator who did the photo manipulation claimed to be unaware that this could be a possible copyright infringement. Yet, *Newsday* had negotiated 175 licenses to use photos with FPG in the past five years.

Rogers v. Koons

This case is perhaps the landmark copyright case in recent history. Each of the attorneys I interviewed mentioned it. I include it here, even though it is not a case involving digital art or media, because of its summary importance in the area of fair use and derivative works.

Art Rogers is a well-known professional photographer. His photographs have been widely exhibited, including at the San Francisco Museum of Modern Art. Rogers' photograph *Puppies* (Figure 8 on page 223) is licensed, along with other works, to Museum Graphics, a company that produces and sells notecards and postcards. Rogers filed against Koons for copyright infringement. Koons did not inform Rogers of his intended use of the photograph *Puppies*.

Jeff Koons is a well-known artist and sculptor whose works are exhibited at galleries and museums in the United States and elsewhere. In preparation for a sculpture exhibit that he called his Banality Show, Koons purchased at least two Museum Graphics notecards with Rogers' *Puppies* photograph. The cards were imprinted with Rogers' copyright notice. Koons tore off the part of the card with the copyright notice and sent the photograph to the Demetz Arts Studio in Italy, with instructions to make a polychromed wood sculptural version of the photograph, a work that Koons instructed Demetz "must be just like the photo." The result is the sculpture shown in Figure 9 on page 223.

chapter eleven

YES, YOU CAN BE SUED OVER A COMP!

Every Art Director's Worst Nightmare

Traditionally, advertising agency art directors have copied a wide range of visual material for preparation of their comps. Some art directors are worried that this practice will come back to haunt them. Now that digital copies are so good, it is more obvious that copying has been done than it was in past years. In the "old days," from the '60s through the '80s, art directors merely traced images in the Lucigraph. Then they would apply color with Magic Markers and otherwise draw in and around an image. It was a lot harder to determine what, exactly, had been copied.

Nowadays every advertising agency art director has access to scanners and artists' and photographers' promotional CD-ROMs and printed promotional materials. Thanks to technology, it's very easy for an art director to use a copyrighted image in a comp. Obviously, these slick new comprehensives aid in the sale of concepts to agency clients. That they may not reduce the market value of the original images is moot. All that really matters is that a copy has been made without permission and that no usage fees were paid to the artist. That's copyright infringement.

The following case deals with a comprehensive, or mock, layout. Take a look at the images in Figures 4 and 5 on page 221, and read the details of the case. Where would you come out on this one?

Still Pending: Tony Stone Images v. Stephen Arscott

Seeking $400,000 in damages, Tony Stone Images sued Stephen Arscott, claiming Arscott illegally copied a photograph by Nick Vedros that was licensed to TSI. Arscott filed his denial in Ontario Court, General Division, in Canada. At the time this book was written, the case was still pending.

The case is interesting in that the alleged copy was for a mock book cover that Arscott entered in the CorelDraw 1994 World Design Contest. Arscott won big in that contest, becoming the Best of Show grand-prize winner. Grand-prize winners in Corel's show typically win both cash prizes and valuable computer hardware. In the long-time tradition of designers, he used "scrap" to create his layout. That is, he literally "drew" on existing visual resources for his layout. But his lawyer said he did not scan the photograph; "He did take a photograph and reproduce it. He made a drawing in CorelDraw, but he did not do anything electronically to infringe TSI's copyright."

Tony Stone Images sees this as a case of blatant copying. Sarah Stone, TSI's director of photography, said the incident "…indicates a need to educate the marketplace in what constitutes infringement, especially in the digital area."

While Corel did not rescind Arscott's Best of Show award, it did avoid using the disputed image in promotional materials. And Corel added fine print to its entry forms to make sure participants in upcoming Corel shows are, indeed, owners of copyright or licensees of all copied artworks. The incident also prompted Corel to sponsor a copyright seminar for graphic designers.

This is a fascinating case in that what amounts to a comprehensive layout received a major prize in an international contest hosted by a major software company. Mock layouts like this do not usually get this kind of public attention or direct monetary compensation. It is unclear whether the mock book cover was used for presentation purposes to a client or whether this was just "an exercise" by Arscott. But the case will probably revolve around how the jury perceives the images and, importantly, whether the usage comes under fair use doctrines. For instance: will the jury decide that there was a substantial "commercial" aspect to this mock layout in that it won a large cash prize? The resolution of this dispute could become one of those precedent-setting cases for which copyright attorneys are waiting.

chapter twelve

BE CAREFUL WHEN YOU SCAN

It's Almost Too Easy to Copy

With scanners, screen-capture programs, and other such tools, it is almost too easy to copy something. Yet naive scanning or copying can land you in court.

The following case hinges on a so-called naive infringement. You have to ask yourself whether or not the art director who did the scan knew that *Newsday* would need to get a license to use the materials.

FPG v. Newsday. Settled Yet Unsettling

In an out-of-court settlement, FPG negotiated a retroactive licensing payment of $20,000—ten times the initial licensing fees—for the disputed use of a photograph by James Porto. FPG was also granted a significant portion of attorneys' fees in its case. And, importantly, FPG is also free to discuss the case. FPG management considers this to be a major win for educational purposes. Now it may use its case to help raise the consciousness of copyright laws in the photography, advertising, publishing, and computer graphics industries.

What is unsettling about this case is the fact that the *Newsday* computer artist scanned James Porto's image from a previously published photo directory, the *1989*

Black Book, Photography. The *Black Book* is one of the most prestigious directories in which photographers promote their work. Even though the image came from a printed page, the *Newsday* staffer was able to manipulate the digital file made from the scan to create a sharp, reproducible image. Obviously any distracting moiré patterns that would have resulted from such a scan were filtered out of the purloined image. Then, the computer artist further edited the image and combined it seamlessly with new elements—digitized photos and a scanned image of yet another photographer, Joe Viesti. No permission was sought in the usage of Viesti's photo, either. The photo collage shown in Figure 7 on page 222 appeared on the cover of *Newsday*'s Long Island edition in November 1993.

That such scans were made in this case is unsettling. As an artist, one hopes that the professional designers and illustrators employed by major publishers are at least minimally aware of copyright laws. But the computer artist who made these scans claimed he was not aware that scanning and reproducing unlicensed photographs might violate the law. This flies in the face of the fact that *Newsday* had previously licensed 175 other photographs from FPG. Barbara Roberts, FPG's president, said, "The idea that millions of published photographs—printed in copyrighted periodicals—may be free for the picking by anyone using a scanner, is a terribly unsettling concept to us, one we believe needed testing in the courts."

Of particular interest in this case is *Newsday*'s claims of fair use. That claim was one of the reasons FPG decided to settle out of court. Roberts said, "Certainly our damage claims would have been stronger had *Newsday* printed the Porto photo onto T-shirts and sold them instead of putting the image to editorial use as front page art to boost sales of the paper." In reference to the settlement, she continued, "It seemed a far better use of our resources to accept a settlement that could allow us to publicly expose the issues in this dispute, while at the same time lobbying actively for changes in the copyright law."

To the distressing issue of scanning, Ms. Roberts said, "Current copyright statutes have been effective in curtailing misuse of photographic transparencies, but the law is woefully weak in dealing with the anonymous abuses that occur with digital scanners." James Porto, in a letter to *Wired* magazine, said, "Curiously, I've noticed that proponents of free usage are people who don't have any of their own images to draw from." An excellent point.

In a final bit of justice, the settlement covered a significant portion of FPG's legal bills. To this point Barbara Roberts said, "One of the biggest stumbling blocks in unauthorized-use cases is the sheer cost of litigation— without the chance for legal fees, who is going to hire a $10,000 attorney to recover $2,000 in licensing fees?"

An interesting postscript: photographer Joe Viesti also received a separate settlement of $15,500 from *Newsday* for the unauthorized scan of his photograph in the same disputed cover story image.

As I researched this book, I contacted several manufacturers of scanners and screen-capture software. I asked some of them if they included some sort of notice in their documentation about it being illegal to copy copyrighted materials. None of them did. A couple of them were actually quite out of joint at my question. One of them testily answered, "That's up to the ethics of our customers and none of our business." Oh? Oh. The Sony Betamax case agrees with the manufacturers. In that case, the U.S. Supreme Court held that the manufacturer of videotape recorders could not be held liable for infringement by the owners of the recorders. The recorder is just a neutral tool; although it makes infringement possible, infringement isn't the only use to which it can be put. But just because something is legal doesn't make it moral.

Manufacturers of scanners, screen-capture software and other related high-tech copying devices are in the perfect position to mount an educational campaign. With their broad distribution, they could reach a tremendous market and help to raise people's consciousness about copying and copyright law.

chapter thirteen

FAIR USE IS NO EXCUSE

Derivative Is Derivative

In the case we might call "The Purloined Puppies," the United States Court of Appeals held for the plaintiff, photographer Art Rogers, against sculptor Jeff Koons. This case is of interest to digital artists because the derivative work that Koons made from Rogers' photograph was a sculpture. It was an image created in a completely different medium from the original image. What the Rogers case demonstrates is that a copy is a copy, and infringement is infringement, regardless of the medium employed in the copying. As such, there are parallels that could have a bearing on artists in the creation of "digital" works from "analog" works. Quoting from the judge's opinion in the case: "In copyright law the medium is not the message, and a change in medium does not preclude infringement." But there are also other salient points to this case that impact the digital artist.

On December 13, 1990, Art Rogers and Jeff Koons met in the United States District Court in New York. At issue was a sculpture by Koons called *String of Puppies* (Figure 9 on page 223). Rogers claimed the sculpture was in violation of his copyrights in his 1980 photograph *Puppies* (Figure 8 on page 223).

The court held in favor of Rogers on two important points and stated:

Reproduction of copyrighted photograph in sculpture form did not preclude finding of copyright infringement; sculpture was derivative work based upon photograph.

Reproduction of copyrighted photograph in sculpture form was not fair use of photograph, where use of photograph did not criticize or comment upon it, was of a commercial nature, and undermined new uses of the photograph.

The evidence against Koons as to whether or not he copied Rogers' photograph was indisputable. Koons gave the Italian artisans who actually created the sculpture one of the notecards he had purchased of Rogers' licensed and copyrighted photograph *Puppies*. In production notes to the artisans, Koons wrote such things as: "work must be just like photo—features of photo must be captured," and, "Puppies need detail in fur. Details—Just Like Photo!" and, "Girl's nose is too small. Please make larger as per photo." There was no doubt that Koons meant to copy Rogers' photo.

Koons never asked Rogers for permission to use the image. And his failure to seek permission was deliberate in that Koons removed Rogers' copyright notice from the notecard. Quoting here from the United States Court of Appeals transcript of the 1991 appeal:

Koons' documents show that he was well aware that he had to obtain permission to use copyrighted material in his works. In numerous prior instances, he had asked for, and obtained, permission to use others' copyrighted material.

What is particularly interesting about this case is what happened when Koons appealed the original verdict. The United States Court of Appeals came out strongly in Rogers' favor, citing fifteen incidents of copyright infringement. In a case that will help to define future copyright infringement cases, the court held that, among other things:

> *Undisputed direct evidence of copying of copyrighted photograph by sculptor, who admittedly gave copy of photograph to artisans and told them to copy it, was sufficient to support entry of summary judgment in photographer's favor on issue of unauthorized copying in copyright infringement action.*

> *Where access to copyrighted work was conceded, and accused work was so substantially similar to copyrighted work that reasonable jurors could not differ on issue, summary judgment on issue of unauthorized copying could be sustained.*

> *Sculptor's* String of Puppies *could not be deemed parody of photographers' photograph for purposes of fair use doctrine where photographer's* Puppies *was not, even in part, object of alleged parody: copied work must be, at least in part, object of parody, otherwise there would be no need to conjure up original work.*

> *Sculptor's claim that his infringement of photographer's work was fair use solely because he was acting within artistic tradition of commenting upon commonplace could not be accepted; copied work was not object of sculptor's parody, as required for protection under fair use doctrine.*

> *Sculptor's unauthorized use of photographer's copyrighted photograph to craft sculpture did not fall under fair use doctrine; among other things, sculptor's intent was to make substantial profit, sculpture could not be considered parody of photograph, photograph was copied nearly in total, sculptor's work was primarily commercial in nature, being produced for sale as high-priced art, and sculpture created likelihood of future harm to market for photographer's work.*

The undisputed facts of the copying were, probably, in and of themselves, enough to support the infringement claims of Rogers. But the judge added significant punch to the verdict in the fair use area as can be seen in the quotes above. Not only did Koons fail to prove fair use as in a parody, but he had publicly asserted that he was in art for the money.

Koons produced his infringing sculpture in a limited edition of four. Three sold to collectors for a total of $367,000. Koons kept the fourth copy. This was obviously a very big business for Koons. Indeed, another aspect of Rogers' case was to have Koons turn over the remaining sculpture as part of the original judgment. In direct violation of that order, and after it was handed down, Koons sent the last copy of the sculpture out of the country to an exhibition in Europe. This did not go unnoticed in the Court of Appeals, which supported a contempt order against Koons.

What the Rogers case means to digital artists is clear: merely lifting an image and moving it into another medium is not a defense. This is simply the creation of a derivative work and not an application of the fair use doctrine. This case also points up the importance of the commercial uses of an allegedly infringing artwork. Will the jury decide that the image clearly cut into the plaintiff's potential market for the copyrighted work? A lot of money was at stake in the Koons copies. Again, fair use is hard to apply in such a situation.

How Did Rogers Find Out about the Infringement?

In one of those serendipitous events, which contains elements of luck and coincidence, a friend of Scanlon's (Scanlon is the man in the Rogers *Puppies* photograph) saw what she thought was a colorized version of *Puppies* on the front page of the calendar section of the May 7, 1989, Sunday *Los Angeles Times*. The "colorized" version was, in fact, the Koons sculpture. It was illustrating an article about its exhibition at the San Francisco Museum of Modern Art. Even in the slower-moving, preelectronic superhighway world, the copyright infringement came to light.

chapter fourteen

SUMMARY AND DISCUSSION

Your Day in Court

While it is comforting to know that such precedent-setting cases are now coming to the aid of artists, it is stressful to face your day in court. The pressures involved in litigation are extreme, and the process, quite literally, takes years. To sustain a clear head and optimistic outlook through depositions, filing, and actual court appearances is challenging. For an artist, these procedures—even if one is the plaintiff with a strong case—can be draining. Even with favorable outcomes, some artists have said that they just want to put their day in court behind them.

I do not write this to completely dissuade you from seeking your day in court if you discover your copyrights have been infringed. I merely want to point out that a lawsuit will be a mental and financial drain. As suggested in Chapter 5, you should seriously consider the extent to which you and your career have been damaged before considering litigation. And, of course, scrupulously observe the copyrights of others so that you do not wind up as the defendant on that day in court. Sitting on *that* side of the courtroom can be even more debilitating.

Back to the Beginning: But Artists Will Copy

As I reviewed these actual cases, I got to thinking about Chapter 1. About the long and rich history of truly great artwork that contains copies of other great works. Hundreds of wonderful artists have copied the works of their predecessors. And these "copies" reside in some of the great collections of the world. It made me more than a little nervous, especially after reviewing some of the actual cases in the preceding chapters.

So I gathered up a file of about a dozen artworks to show to a couple of the copyright attorneys I interviewed. My question to the attorneys was this: how would each of these "copied" images stand up in a court of law? Here are samples of some of the answers.

Is Helga Like Mona?

For this exercise I made a color copy of the book cover of Andrew Wyeth's *The Helga Pictures*. Then I painted a mustache and goatee on the beautiful Helga. I also painted out Andrew Wyeth's name and added my own name with a copyright symbol. I asked if this would be considered to be a "fair use" if my concept were to mock both the painting and the pretensions of a book of fine art paintings. Or would my "artwork" constitute a sort of double whammy copyright infringement: first for copying the book cover, then for producing a derivative work? Was this the same thing as Duchamp putting the mustache on a poster of Mona Lisa or not?

The answer was "yes." Conceptually it is the same kind of artwork as the Duchamp *Mona Lisa*. Here's why. In my deliberate defacement I poked fun at the formalism of the Wyeth work, at the concept of the beautiful woman as subject matter, and at the pretensions of the art book. And so it would probably be judged to be a form of parody and would fall under fair use doctrines. And it uses the original work as a clear reference point for my conceptual comments.

If, however, I had painted a copy of the Helga portrait and merely added some gray hairs to make her appear older, that copy would probably *not* fall under fair use doctrines. Let's say that I held that I was commenting satirically on the idea of *the male painter's obsession with beautiful women as subject matter*. The attorneys felt that such a work would probably not pass the Judge's Test. It would appear that I was just too lazy to come up with my own interpretation of the idea of *the male painter's obsession with beautiful women as subject matter*.

Dalí Copied the Whole Thing— Surely That's an Infringement!

In Chapter 1 I referred to Dalí's homage to Millet's *Angelus*. Here is a case where a painter copied *the entire work* of another artist in his derivative work. Surely, in terms of today's copyright laws, this work would end up in court, right? Well, probably not. According to the opinions of the attorneys interviewed, this great Dalí work would pass both the Judge's Test and exceptions to copyrights in the original. Here's why. (And let's assume that Millet's painting is not in the public domain, although it is. Let's also assume that Dalí scanned a copyrighted magazine reproduction of the painting for use in his work. These assumptions make the discussion a lot more interesting—and relevant.)

The copy in this composition is used as the reference point to a greater statement by the artist, Dalí. He has surrounded the copy with a great deal of interpretive visualization from his own creative imagination and, as such, he creates an homage to the original image. Dalí adds elements of his subconscious to the homely farm scene. He extends and augments the original in a way that redefines the understanding of the original in the viewer's mind. The Judge's Test observes the extent to which the artist who copies has gone to create his own *idea* of the *Angelus.* Dalí was not "just too lazy" to come up with his own concept. He used the Millet image as source for a much greater idea. He also commented on it, visually and iconographcally. Remember that fair use identifies comment as one of the purposes that will support fair use.)

Is This Case Like Rogers v. Koons?

Now, this case, on the surface, is much like the puppy dog postcard v. the puppy sculpture—except for a few critically important points. In 1967 Magritte created this bronze sculpture based on the work *Madame Recamier,* painted by Jacques-Louis David in 1800. Magritte made his three-dimensional derivative sculpture from a two-dimensional artwork just as in the *Rogers v. Koons* case. But this case, and Dalí/Millet, could not be *less* like *Rogers v. Koons.*

Of course, the David image was in the public domain, as was the Millet. But more important for our analysis, Magritte's work is a true parody. Why is his sculpture a parody? In order to qualify as parody, the "copy" must make clear reference to the original work of art. A reasonable judge must be able to see that the artist has copied another artist's work of art. But they must also be able to observe that the "copy-ist" took a conceptual step beyond the original image. Certainly it is clear that Magritte put an ironic twist on the classical elegance of the original *Madame Recamier.* In a somewhat chilling visual pun, Magritte has spoofed both the original artist and his lovely subject. This sculpture goes way beyond a mere copy of the *idea* of a lovely lady on her lounge. It goes well beyond the specific *image* of *this* lovely lady on her lounge. It is a completely different and original work of art that comments on and pokes fun at the recognizable original from which it is derived. That's the essence of parody.

FOR WHAT IT's WORTH...

Legal Example
United States Court of Appeals for the Second Circuit, 91-7396. Art Rogers, Plaintiff-Appellee-Cross-Appellant, against Jeff Koons and Sonnabend Gallery, Inc., Defendants-Appellants-Cross-Appellees.

Radio Transcript
"Copyright in the Electronic Age," Transcript of Program #3-94, KPFA's Communications Revolution series.

WHERE DO WE GO FROM HERE?

chapter fifteen

ENFORCEMENT: PROTECTING YOUR COPYRIGHTS WITH TECHNOLOGY

This chapter provides a quick tour of the technology that is either currently available, or very soon to be, that can help digital artists protect their digitized work from copyright infringement, in digital file formats such as CD-ROM, or on the Net.

Portable-Document Programs: Your First Line of Defense

As an artist, the first thing you will probably consider doing is to self-publish. Whether you opt to do this on CD-ROM, a bulletin-board system online, or as a color fax-back service for clients or prospects, you will need to create a document that will remain visually stable no matter what the system at the receiving end. To do this your electronically published document will need to contain all of the building blocks of the document—the fonts, the graphics, and a program viewer or reader. You will need a portable-document program to convert your QuarkXPress or PageMaker design.

Portable-document programs come with a variety of features including the ability to accurately reproduce, at the receiver's end, TIFF, EPS, or PICT files and all the fonts you use in your electronic documents.

Of the leading products in the portable-document category—Adobe Acrobat Exchange, Replica, and Common Ground—only the latter two offer the artist some degree of copy protection for images. Common Ground has a feature that prevents recipients from printing files or copying text or graphics. Replica can restrict a recipient to read-only. Each of these programs works with QuarkXPress and PageMaker with varying degrees of success. You first do your page layout using Quark, for instance, then use your portable-document software when preparing your files.

There are many other features to assess when considering a portable-document program, such as topic search features, font fidelity, document annotation, and the degree of control you have over image resolution. But if it's the security of your images you seek, the first question to ask tech support before you make a purchase is, "Does this portable-document program offer a read-only option, and can I prevent recipients from copying, downloading, or printing my files?" If so, then you have provided your images with their first line of defense against infringement along the electronic superhighway.

New, New, New, and Pretty Secure, Too

If you are thinking of creating your own fax-on-request newsletter and want to provide some security for your document to assure that it reaches the right party, you might try a product called 3D FAX from InfoImaging Technologies, Inc. This brand-new product offers many powerful tools such as compression to save transmission time, color multimedia faxing capability that includes sound and full-motion video transmission, and password protection. Password protection, while not the same as encryption, will at least provide you with some measure of control over the destination of your electronically published images. Since faxed images are going point-to-point, not over the Internet, there is no possibility of the work being intercepted and pirated en route. With password protection, the receiving party has to unlock the digital file with a password before the file can be viewed. Worth looking into.

HTML—Standard on the Web, but No Security Support

With the World Wide Web, you no longer require the auspices of a professional publishing enterprise to assemble, market, and distribute your work to a vast marketplace. It's a forum that is hungry for creativity and newness.

The standard tool for creating a Web page is called HTML—Hypertext Markup Language. HTML lets you create a Web page document that can be linked with a wide variety of visual and text elements. For instance, you can include a short biography and highlight the name of the gallery where you had your last show. With HTML you can link to the gallery's web site to show some of your paintings that are on display there. Or if you use a particular brand of acrylic paint, you could have a link to that manufacturer's Web page for more technical information.

But, as of this writing, HTML tools provide *no* security for your images. Graphics and text are wide open to anybody out there. You must assume that not only are people linking to your images, but that there may also be some downloading of your images from those linked sites. And once the images are downloaded, it's impossible at this point to determine whether or not your copyrights are being infringed by the person who does the downloading.

But you should not jump to the conclusion that this vulnerability of your images necessarily precludes your use of a Web page. Many digital artists use their home page to "sample" their work to the vast networked audience. They put lower resolution, smaller images on their home pages or use images that are not their most valuable ones. It can be an excellent way to expand your reach, to receive feedback, and, eventually, you may even want to put your images into one of the online catalogs or malls for direct marketing. I strongly recommend that you get involved in designing your own home page and that, for the time being, you relax your copyrights in this setting. By this I mean: pursue only those infringers who copy and try to market your images as their own. Do not pursue the kids who copy your images to keep or show to friends as examples of "cool" artwork.

HTML tools are available as freeware, shareware, and in commercial applications. For the creation of my Chicken Lady Web site I used HTML Assistant Pro and LView Pro, which are both shareware programs and are fairly straightforward to use.

Digital Watermarks—Safe and Pretty Easy

One of the easiest ways to protect a digital image is with a digital watermark. With a digital watermark on your CD-ROM, diskette, or SyQuest images, your client can view your image on screen but will not be able to print the image without the watermark showing up. For instance, digital watermarks can protect your work during the initial stages of development of an illustration. You want your clients to be able to look at the illustration, but, at this point, you do not want them to be able to reproduce the illustration. Digital watermarks are also good for portfolios of work you place on CD-ROM, diskette, or SyQuest disks. People may review the work and see it displayed on their monitors, but they will not be able to reproduce your work on paper. For instance, if an art director wanted to use one of your portfolio images on a comprehensive, the watermark would show up on the printout of the piece.

Here's how to place a watermark on your work.

1. Make a CMYK separation of your image.

2. On the cyan sep put a translucent "mark" on the center of the image. This mark can be your name, your logo, or any other symbol you choose. Be sure to place the mark so that it covers enough of your image so that it cannot be cropped out.

That's all there is to it. You now have an image that is safe from the casual infringer. While it's still possible to undo this kind of lock, you will at least discourage most image pirates as they would have to go to considerable trouble to re-create the cyan plate of your image. You may produce digital watermarks in photo-manipulation programs and in bit-mapped and vector drawing programs. The watermarked image may be saved as a CMYK TIFF file.

Pretty Good Privacy: Free Encryption Software Available On-Line

No longer the stuff of super-secret spy rings, encryption has moved well into the domain of the everyday computer user. This is the story of one man's genius in the development of a super-sophisticated lock for any kind of digital file. It is the story of giving it away free on the Net. It is, unfortunately, a story with an uncertain ending. However, for artists, Pretty Good Privacy encryption software is just that, pretty (darned) good.

What is it? PGP is a form of public-key encryption. It can be used on any digital file, on text or graphics. You may apply it to your digitally produced images in EPS, TIFF, JPEG, and any other file formats you use. Public-key encryption refers to the fact that it uses one key to encode a file (the so-called public key, your key) and one key to decode it (for instance, your client's key). The system is incredibly safe at this point in time, and impervious to cracking, hacking, pirating, and pillaging. Highly recommended as a safeguard for your images online.

There is just one small problem. Nobody but your intended viewer can see your image. This may serve your purposes to a tee. Or it might seem like an unnecessary limitation on the availability of your images for public viewing. You decide.

Your Proverbial Hornet's Nest

Philip Zimmerman, a mild-mannered professorial-type data security consultant, built the most powerful encryption program in the land, a truly elegant thing he modestly called Pretty Good Privacy, and distributed it free on the Net. Then all hell broke loose: he was held in possible violation of federal arms-export laws, and a San Jose grand jury started gathering evidence on him. Never mind that the Electronic Frontier Foundation awarded him its prestigious Pioneer Award—his genius and generosity could have earned him a big stretch behind bars. But the story ended happily. In January 1996 the U.S. Attorney's office decided *not* to prosecute Zimmerman for the international export of PGP.

PGP is available for personal and noncommercial use, free, online. Just use anonymous ftp to connect with net-dist.mit.edu and switch to the directory /pub/PGP. Download the README file for instructions. Or you can obtain it for commercial use, for a fee, from ViaCrypt, 2104 West Peoria Avenue, Phoenix, AZ 85029. Phone: 602/944-0773.

Warning: PGP is still export-restricted by the Office of Export Administration, United States Department of Commerce, and the Offices of Defense Trade Controls and Munitions Control, United States Department of State.

Yes, Master

As of this writing, a lot of technology visionaries are working on various forms of artificial intelligence. And lest this sound too futuristic for common consumption, a lot of scientists believe that software "agents" will be a thing of the very near future.

Currently at MIT, researchers are working on agents to help people find and retrieve information in the labyrinths of the Net. This could mean that within the next couple of years you would be able to install a software agent into your personal system and let that agent track the Net for unauthorized downloading of your copyrighted images. The agent would provide you with a list of the Net "addresses" where images were downloaded so that you could employ another agent to send those persons a cease and desist letter. If this sounds too implausible, consider this: there are already such things going on in the Internet Relay Chat service. Over there, they are called *Bots* and they roam around in that cyberspace performing a variety of useful or annoying chores for their "masters." So this form of weird science is already up and running.

ON THE OTHER HAND...

Then again, what are we talking about here when we talk about protecting art images with cryptography? I mean, this is not the world of high finance or sensitive medical records or atomic weaponry. We're talking art. Pictures. Images. Objects to raise our souls from the drab mire of philistinism. Truth. Beauty. And all that. Just how protected do your images really need to be?

Mind Your Business on the Net

As of this writing, technologies for safe money transactions online are becoming widely available. What this means to the artist is that you can offer your work for sale on the Net.

What this is, is a form of public-key encryption. Very safe. I anticipate a day when artists and photographers could put a portfolio onto a CD, distribute copies of the CD to clients and prospects, then monitor usage and receive payments using this newest technology. And, very soon, it will also be possible to market work on the Net and to receive payment electronically through virtual banks. Such banks are in place right now; however you can only sell electronic goods, not hard goods, at this point in time. But just wait a day or so.

ON THE OTHER HAND...

But how would you know if the person who downloaded your image went further with it? How would you know whether or not someone was just looking at your image or actually putting it on posters and selling it? Technology may be able to find copying, but it will never be able to evaluate the impact of the copying on me or my career.

But It Only Goes So Far

Regardless of the sophistication of some of these forms of protection, each one presents you with limitations and risks. For example, if you decide to encrypt your images, you will limit your potential to attract viewers because only the viewer with the key will be able to see your images. If you decide to produce read-only files for your electronically produced documents, you still run the risk of screen-capture software. And anyone can download and copy a Web image. Anyone can scan an existing printed piece. Technology can only go so far helping you protect and enforce your copyrights in cyberspace.

FOR WHAT IT'S WORTH...

Book

The Computer Privacy Handbook
By Andre Bacard
Peachpit Press
2414 Sixth Street
Berkeley, CA 94710
510/548-4393
ISBN 1-56609-171-3

Learn all about encryption. An in-depth study about how and why to lock things in the digital age.

Magazines

For up-to-date information about electronic publishing software and digital watermarks and encryption you should read as many of these magazines as possible: *PC* magazine, *Publish, Wired, Microtimes, Computer Currents*. At the very least, skim them at your library.

Organizations

Computer Professionals for
Social Responsibility

Electronic Frontier Foundation

ON THE OTHER HAND...

You can already see the polyvisual universe into which your work will flow. You have only to spend an afternoon at a large bookstore, stroll the hallways of a couple of museums, Net-surf a few hundred Web sites, thumb through a few thousand 'zines, do the clubs, browse in your clients' brochure files, go to the movies, watch 500 channels of television. You have only to open your eyes a little bit to see the gorgeous and nauseating overabundance of images. Bacterializing images, like electrons and ergs, like the proverbial grains of sand on the seashore. Images are proliferating in boggling densities. By the day, by the hour, the nanosecond. Nobody will ever see them all. Who will police this world of images breeding like germs? Who will know about the artist who infringes? Or protect the artist who has been infringed?

chapter sixteen

SAFETY: USING ROYALTY-FREE ART

How to Own Every Square Inch of Your Own Work

Now the fun part. If you are an artist who works in montage or collage or in any form of multimedia, you have many resources at your command. Technology provides you with the locks, and technology also provides you with the assurances. The digital image marketplace offers you an enormous and growing stockpile of royalty-free images so that you can be assured that your work will not infringe the copyrights of others. Most of these collections come on CD-ROMs, and the digital quality is very high. The files are fully editable, and images may be imported into your vector or bit-mapped drawing or photo-manipulation programs.

There is only one proviso: you'll be using this material subject to the license that the manufacturer grants you, so read the manufacturer's advertising carefully. If it does not include the words *royalty-free*, the images might require you to pay per usage. And in some cases the words *royalty-free* are boldface in the ad, but exceptions are listed in the small print. Call before purchasing, if you are uncertain. Sometimes even royalty-free collections can't be used for commercial purposes. Subject to limitations of that kind, any image collection that says it contains royalty-free images means that you may use any of the images for just the price of the collection. And, believe me, these collections are priced very competitively. Almost all artists can afford to have a few of them in their scrap files. By using royalty-free elements in your work, you can rest assured that you have the license to the usage of the images in your own original collage, montage, or multimedia creations. Copyright in the royalty-free elements still belongs to the owner who licensed you the right to use it in your work.

The Best Resources

Please turn to Appendix G for a list and review some of my favorite royalty-free image collections.

chapter seventeen

SURVIVAL: GIVING YOUR ART AWAY AND MAKING A LIVING

The Bottom Line

While this entire book is written to help artists understand and cope with copyrights in the digital era, this particular chapter focuses on what is, at bottom, the most important issue for artists and their copyrights: the bottom line. This chapter focuses on making a living.

While most artists would rather be making art than worrying about it, there is one overriding concern: how can I make a living in the digital era? If *anyone* can copy *anything, any time, any place,* how am I going to get paid for my work?

At a glance, the issue of remuneration for the work seems to be tied to copyright law. Without your copyrights, how will you be able to enforce payment for your work? But, consider for a moment the logistics of just three payment schemes: pay-per-view, royalties, and entrepreneurship.

Pay-Per-View

Will end users and home consumers pay for images they view using a pay-per-view system, for instance? How will views be monitored? Who will collect the money from each viewing? How will the money get into the artist's pocket? What constitutes a chargeable view? Just looking at something? Downloading it?

Of course, there's another critically important question here, too. How will a consumer know, in advance of viewing, the value of what he or she is going to be charged for? The consumer sees a list of pay-per-view sites and reads: The oeuvre of unknown artist Mary E. Carter? Pass.

Royalties

Let's say the networks and BBS operators, in a kind of royalty scheme, provide for payment to artists for usage of images on their systems. Once again, who will monitor and collect the royalties? What will constitute a chargeable view? Are network or BBS systems equipped with the bookkeeping departments required for such a monumental task?

Entrepreneurship

Will all artists become entrepreneurs? Many of them are already. You put your work out there on your home page. For sale. How are you going to monitor usage and put a value on on-line usages? Will you have the tools to help you track downloading of your images? And, if so, will you charge a usage fee when a teenager downloads your image just to look at it?

The logistics for any of these schemes are boggling. It's time to look at your copyrights from a completely different perspective.

Intellectual Property: Mine, Mine, Mine

When I started research for this book, I was convinced that I would never give up a single iota of my copyrights. Utterly appalled by the suggestions by some technological visionaries that copyright law should be discarded, my attitude was, "I'll never budge on *my* sacred copyrights." Then I began reading the work of Esther Dyson, which suggested a radically different perspective on this copyright animal, one rooted in economic practicality. Copyright law, after all, rests on an economic foundation.

As outlined in the Constitutional framework of copyright law, the artist maintains a temporary monopoly on the sale and distribution of her artwork. So when we talk copyrights we automatically talk economics. Sales and distribution. Pricing. Marketing and promotion. All of the corollary activities that go into the economic life of an artwork.

Then, too, remember this: copyright laws are among the many civil laws that are *optional*. A citizen-artist has the option *not* to enforce his own copyrights. Unlike traffic laws that protect drivers. Or laws prohibiting murder that support a civilized social contract. Copyright laws are tools to help the artist maintain value for artwork in the marketplace. *If* the artist chooses to enforce them. Well, well.

Since copyright laws have their foundation in economics, let's explore them in this light. What are the economic consequences of *not* enforcing copyrights on the Net? In her newsletter *Release 1.0*, published 28 December 1994, Esther Dyson wrote these words, and they hit home:

> *The Net poses interesting challenges both for owners/creators/sellers and for users of intellectual property. Because it allows for essentially costless copying of*

content, it dramatically changes the economics of content...The problem for providers of intellectual property is that although under law they can control the pricing of their own products, they will operate in an increasingly competitive marketplace where much intellectual property is distributed free and the number of suppliers is exploding...The likely best defense for content providers [read: artists] *is to exploit that situation—to distribute intellectual property free in order to sell services and relationships. The provider's task is to figure out what to charge for and what to give away for free.... This is not a moral decision but a business strategy.*

Free samples. It's ingeniously simple. Candy makers have been giving away free samples forever, the strategy being to hook the candy eater into making purchases that will far exceed the investment in the sampling. Service providers, like your local bricklayer, have long given free estimates. The idea here has always been that the free advice leads to the contract for the work. Even software manufacturers, with their enormous investments in R&D, are now giving away free samples and even encouraging the copying of their programs, once sacrosanct in copyright-protection constraints. How many bars of soap have appeared in your mailbox, free? How many coupons have you clipped for a free pizza? Free sampling of value-added goods and services is an old and reliable sales technique.

So why haven't artists done much of this? Logistics is one reason. But the electronic superhighway changes all this. Suddenly we have a medium, for the first time in technological history, through which an artist can realistically distribute free samples of the work to a vast potential marketplace. By choice, the samples can go out there free of copyright constraint. Protecting your copyright is optional. You are, in fact, foolish if you obsess about your copyrights in that environment for, as we have observed, bandits lurk around every corner. It's not a bad idea to let a potential user know that you own the copyright, and that you grant a limited license for further use, even for the creation of derivative works. At least you maintain some semblance of control, modified to take account of the realities of electronic life.

The electronic superhighway is a vast and fertile showcase for the working artist. And sooner or later the paying work will come round. Sampling can be problematic for the artist because in this new economic model the artist must now figure out what, exactly, to give away, and what to charge for. But Ms. Dyson supplies at least part of the answer as she continues in that same December newsletter:

> *Frustratingly to creators...the value of their work doesn't generally get recognized without broad distribution. This means that any artist or creator must somehow attract broad attention to attract high payment for copies—which means you give the first performances, books, or whatever away in hopes of recouping with subsequent works...People want to pay for that which is scarce—a personal performance or a custom application, for example, or some tangible manifestation... that's why we have numbered lithographs....*

Ms. Dyson's economic model reasserts the value of the hand-crafted object, long the pride of the artist. The artist in the digital era has a new method of broad distribution and sampling for her work—the electronic superhighway. Then, once she has established her reputation, the artist can manufacture more precious works for narrower distribution and sales. Or, if she is a performance artist, she can sample the work on-line, free, and charge for the actual real-time performances. The digital era provides the best of big-time advertising "reach" with the exclusivity (and hence high market value) of the limited-edition artwork. It is such an elegant concept. Neat and simple.

The Bottom Line?

If you give a little you will get a lot. Put some of your work on-line. Make a Web site with samples of your work. Realize that your copyrights will be very hard, if not impossible, to enforce out there. But realize, too, that you will probably reap rewards from the sampling. Know when to charge the "full ticket" for your work. When a client calls because she has just viewed your artwork on-line, be prepared to wheel and deal to your—and your copyrights'—best advantage. See the next chapter to find out what's in the fine print.

FOR WHAT IT'S WORTH...

Newsletter

Esther Dyson's Monthly Report Release 1.0
EDVenture Holdings, Inc.
104 Fifth Avenue, 20th Floor
New York, NY 10011
$595 per year and worth every penny

This monthly newsletter provides readers with Esther Dyson's unique take on the Net. She is one of the key thinkers of the era and well worth investing with your hard-earned dollars and valuable time. Her views on making a living on the Net and corollary issues about intellectual property are important to the professional artist.

chapter eighteen

FINE PRINT: ARTISTS' REPS' TIPS FOR WHEELING AND DEALING WITH CONTRACTS

Protecting Your Copyrights on Paper

While this is not a book about how to construct a contract, I will highlight some of the more important things to watch for when you start reading the fine print. Signing a contract along the electronic superhighway can be hazardous. For professional graphic designers, illustrators, and photographers there are many pitfalls. You can lose your copyrights in many old-fashioned situations. And you can lose your copyrights in a whole new set of "digital" situations. Plus, there's more than just copyrights at stake every time you sign a contract. Don't forget that working with contracts in the digital era is still the same as it was in the "olden" days. You are still negotiating terms for the scope of usage for the images you license; terms for payment; terms for kill fees; and the terms for the project's management (due dates, and so on). It's the same old world of business as usual.

For the tips here, I interviewed a half dozen top artists' representatives, each of them in the business for more than ten years. These folks are down in the trenches, every day. They read and negotiate contracts for their artists, compose letters of agreement, and handle disputes. The best artists' reps know copyright law backwards and forwards and can hold their own in conversations with copyright attorneys. They also understand and manage all other aspects of the basic artists' contract—from change orders to indemnification clauses. They are staunch defenders of their artists, a cross between mother hens and father confessors. Here is what they have to say about artists' contracts.

Contract Watch: Artists' Reps Top Ten Tips

1. Beware of work-made-for-hire provisions.

Warning: You usually give up all rights when you do work made for hire.

This is important. You do not own your original artwork or your copyrights to it when you produce "work made for hire" or "work for hire." (These phrases mean the same thing.) This work is contracted for in two ways; for the details, see Chapter 2.

- You, the creator of the work, are an employee of a firm or person, and creating the work made for hire is part of your job.

- You, the creator of the work, are an independent contractor, but the client comes to you and orders or commissions the work. You and the client both sign a written agreement—it can be your client's project contract, or purchase order—which states that your work is "made for hire" or "work for hire" or uses equivalent words

2. Beware of conflicting purchase orders.

Sometimes a client will issue a purchase order many days or weeks after a project is under way. You might have signed a contract at the outset of the project that you are happy with, but the purchase order might contain new or different terms from your contract. Do not sign a purchase order that has terms you do not agree to. Sometimes purchase orders contain work-for-hire provisions. Strike them out, initial the strike-throughs, and discuss your objections with the project manager or art director.

3. Deal with the person in charge—and get signatures.

Make sure the person who authorizes you to strike out or make changes on a contract or purchase order has the authority to do so. There are many cases where art directors have said to an artist, "Sure, go ahead and cross out any provisions you don't agree to." Then, later, an account manager or company attorney says that the art director did not have the authority to make changes in the "standard" contract. Determine ahead of time who has the authority to let you make changes to a contract or purchase order and negotiate with that person. And make sure that person—or some authorized person—initials and signs contracts and contract changes. If they're important enough to warrant changes on the paperwork, they're important enough to warrant the nuisance of getting them documented with initials and signatures.

4. Hold onto your copyrights.

You may negotiate the licensing of your image in *many* or *few* situations. Do not sell all the parts of your copyright to an image unless the client really needs them and you are adequately compensated for them. Spell out the exact usages for your artwork, put them in writing in the contract or purchase order, and set your fees accordingly. It is better to sell limited usage of your work than to sell all rights.

5. Make sure your client understands what is meant by the words *total buyout*.

A total buyout means that the client licenses the images for unlimited use *in the category in which you sold it*. It *does not* include a transfer of copyrights for usage in any other situation. Put this in writing on your contract or letter of agreement.

For example: you sell fifty spot illustrations for usage in an educational manual that teaches children about computers. You license your client to usages that include a total buyout of your images for the educational manual, a poster that accompanies the educational manual, and promotional materials for the manual. Your client may not use the images in their television advertising for their computer hardware.

6. Retain ownership of your original artwork.

Do not sell your original artwork to your client. If you must do so, make sure that you receive adequate remuneration. In the analog days of paint on canvas, what constituted the original was pretty obvious. But in the digital era, what constitutes the "original" may be harder to pin down. At the end of a project a digital artist hands over a diskette or SyQuest disk to the client for reproduction. Is this the original? Yes. Since each digital file is identical to the so-called original file on your hard drive, each "copy" acts as an original. And, theoretically, anyone can make changes to the file. Make sure your contract has a provision for the return of your artwork on diskette or SyQuest disk once your client has made film or separations from it. Of course, anyone can make a copy of this on a hard drive, so your "original" digital file may get *stored* in someone else's hard drive. This is one of the facts of life for digital artists that makes holding onto original

ON THE OTHER HAND...

Try never to sign anything that starts with the word witnesseth. I mean, really, who are they trying to bamboozle? All those whereases and therefores. Are we artists or are we lawyers? What happened to the old-fashioned phone call and a handshake? I just read a "Consultant Services Agreement" that was handed to an artist friend of mine— nine pages of legal bilge water, including this: the corporation (which shall remain nameless because I'm such a nice guy) wanted to run a credit check on this artist.

What???!!! Jeez.

digital artwork a very iffy proposition. So include a provision in your contract that allows one copy for backup or archiving, but no uses except those specified in the contract. A Better Handy Hint for keeping your original digital artwork: put a provision in your contract that says you will provide the client with film as the final art and that you, the artist, shall retain the original digital files. (This will give you more quality control, too, as you can use your favorite service providers and supervise the process.)

ON THE OTHER HAND...

Well, we're up against it: the effects of living in a fragmented culture, where social pressure doesn't seem to matter. So what does matter? A provable contract, with details and signatures. It's just part of the cost of doing business, a most unpleasant part for artists, but no less necessary. It's a good idea to insist that things be clear, well-defined, and as comprehensive as your experience with deadbeat clients, or those who change and change and change again, and don't want to pay for the changes, or those who claim rights you never sold them, dictates. Sad but true. 🐂

7. Spell out kill fees.

You will need a provision in your contract that specifies the amount and circumstances for kill fees. Generally it is standard practice in contracts to say that an artist gets a 50 percent kill fee if a client cancels the project (for any reason whatsoever) before completion of the artwork; and 100 percent of the fee if the project is canceled after completion of the artwork.

8. Specify who can make changes to the artwork.

This term is particularly important to the digital artist. When you hand over a diskette with your artwork on it, it is all too easy for a client to change it. Everybody has the same illustration and photo-manipulation programs. One of the things that makes it so tempting to alter digital artwork is that you will never completely ruin it. You can hit undo or make a backup file before trying to alter it. In analog days, it was by far more difficult for an art director to change a painting or piece of stipple art, for instance. Because of this, you should have a term in your contract that states that only you, the artist, may make changes to the artwork. You might even want to put a financial deterrent in your contract: if your client changes your digital artwork, the fee is triple.

9. Watch out for indemnification clauses.

In this day and age of sometimes frivolous litigation, companies are trying to lay the burden of responsibility for lawsuits onto the shoulders of the artist. An indemnification clause can take many forms, but typically it says that the artist takes full responsibility for the originality of the image she creates *and* for any disputes arising out of the use of the image. This can include holding the client harmless for the artwork once it goes into the public view. On the surface, there is certainly nothing wrong with guaranteeing to your client that you did not copy anyone else's artwork. But there can be complications.

What if an artist decides your image looks a lot like one of his images and sees that your client is Mr. Deep Pockets? The artist initiates a frivolous lawsuit, figuring he will be able to retire on the judgment. Meanwhile, you have signed an indemnification clause with your client Mr. Deep Pockets. You are alone in this. Your client says, "Tough luck, kid," and you are left alone to defend yourself, solely responsible for hiring, and paying for, your own attorney. This is not paranoia. These things can happen. You will see many indemnification clauses in contracts. Try to avoid them. Then again, if you can't, you might want to look into "errors and omissions" insurance, either by getting your own or by being a named additional insured on your client's policy (which should cost nothing extra).

10. Watch out for overly broad electronic rights buyouts.

Watch out for any wording that says you license your copyrights to your work in any and/or all electronic media. This is particularly important for artists who work in traditional media and for projects that are traditional venues for artwork—ads, television graphics and cartooning, brochures, and so on. Clients may want to convert your work into digital formats, including Web pages or other electronic documents. Be especially cautious about wording that states that you license your copyrights in "any electronic media, now known or yet to be invented, in the known universe." If you think this is a joke, read the fine print on some of those contracts out there. Make sure that your contract specifies which electronic usages you are licensing and make sure you are compensated for each usage. For instance you could license your image for use as a printed poster, a brochure cover, and a Web page and charge a separate fee for each of those usages.

11. Specify arbitration or mediation terms.

In addition to the above considerations, you may want to include a provision in your contract about arbitration and mediation. Some of your clients' contracts will already contain such provisions. Read the terms and conditions thoroughly. Ask if you may add such a term if it is not already in the contract. Specify which arts and mediation services you want, by name, and, if you are working for a client out of state, specify which state you prefer for arbitration.

"Never Eat Anything Bigger Than Your Head"

The cartoonist Kliban penned that line under one of his famous cartoons and it was the title for one of his acerbic little books. The same could be said for contracts nowadays. Never sign anything longer than a page.

Yeah, sure! Unfortunately, adhering to this advice is well nigh impossible.

Not only is this the digital era, it is the era of the bloated contract. Many are the artist and rep who have been presented with ten pages of six-point boilerplate. This is enough to send even the sanguine over the top. One rep said to me, "If it takes a lawyer to interpret it, it's not a good contract." You should not have to retain a staff attorney in order to function as an artist in the business world. Sadly, many contracts have grown out of all reasonable proportions. I have one client who sends me a five-page purchase order for a $75 scan. Many clients will state flatly that these are "standard contracts" and hand you the pen. There is no such thing as a "standard contract."

All I can say here to sum up is, be aware of the terms and conditions on the contracts you sign. Put terms that you require into writing. Avoid signing "standard contracts." Read anything you sign before you sign. And, if it is too confusing, call an attorney for advice. And, if you have a good artists' rep, treat her to lunch. She's worth every penny.

ON THE OTHER HAND...

This is why I have a rep. I am constitutionally incapable of dealing with this kind of legalistic paper-slinging without blowing a fuse. Reps are so cool. They can charm their way out of all kinds of unutterable contract terms and conditions. And they do it behind the scenes so I don't have to get all nervous and jerky about it. It's so soothing knowing Barb is out there, fighting my battles for me. Hey, girl, go to it! 🐂

FOR WHAT IT's WORTH...

Books

Graphic Artists Guild Handbook: Pricing & Ethical Guidelines
Graphic Artists Guild
11 W. 20th Street
New York, NY 10011-3704
212/463-7730

The definitive source for contractual terms and conditions. Very detailed information for each of many art specialties. A must for the professional artist.

Multimedia Law Handbook
By J. Dianne Brinson and Mark F. Radcliffe
Ladera Press
3130 Alpine Road, Suite 200-9002
Menlo Park, CA 94025
800/523-3721
ISBN 0-9639173-0-7

A useful, detailed sourcebook for multimedia artists. Contains form contracts, licensing agreements, model releases, nondisclosure forms, and many other types of forms and contracts at the back of the book. Excellent reference. Should be on your bookshelf, well dog-eared.

chapter nineteen

IT'S ART. BUT IS IT JUST INFORMATION? MAKING ETHICAL CHOICES

Outlaws, Iconoclasts, the Good, the Bad, the Possible, and Intellectual Property

There is a vociferous crowd of people who do not think copyright laws will work in the digital era. I've talked about some of these people in Chapter 7. Among them are the technocentrists who believe that many of the conventional rules of society will have to be reconsidered as society moves more of its activities into the realm of cyberspace. For many such thinkers, the phrase "information wants to be free" reflects a well considered or even deeply philosophical perspective. Unfortunately, for every deep thinker pondering the future of virtual communities, there are more than a few garden-variety criminals for whom "information wants to be free" is simply a rationalization for freely appropriating things that are not theirs.

Compounding the problem is the general ignorance of a large crowd who might be termed "innocents"—net-surfing families with kids who copy art off the Net without fully being aware of the rules of copyright; and manufacturers whose products—scanners and screen-capture software, for instance—could become the idiot savant hardware accomplices to intellectual property thefts.

It starts out innocently enough.

A cozy American family sits down at the computer terminal one evening for a bit of familial net-surfing. They stumble into an "art gallery" and see a virtual roomful of wonderful artwork. The kids are stoked. Mom and Dad are clearly delighted. So they download about a hundred wonderful images into their own computer's hard drive.

Copyright infringement number one: technically this is a copyright infringement. Only the artist has the exclusive right to copy the artwork, and storing a version on hard disk is making a copy. But the use is strictly for the family's private enjoyment, so, (a) no one's going to know about it; (b) by putting the image on the Net, the person postering it made it available for storage and may even have licensed that kind of copying; and (c) the damages are probably immeasurably small. But wait.

This is fun! It's also really easy for the kids to "play with" the images—and even to use them in their own artwork. Now we're a little closer to the real thing: infringement by making unauthorized derivative works. Still, the works are purely for fun at home. This is more like the art student copying Picasso at the Museum of Modern Art.

Take it a step further: the kids use the images in school reports. Still no problem. This is almost certainly fair use. And another step: the kids make posters to sell to their friends. Now we've reached the point at which fun becomes something else.

Meanwhile, Mom wants to use these images on T-shirts for her small town's summer bazaar. She figures she can have the T-shirts made up for about $5 each and can sell them for about $12. She could well afford the booth fee and make a nice profit to boot.

Is this OK? Or is this electronic highway robbery?

This is Electronic Highway Robbery. This is clearly a case of copyright infringement. Mom is affecting the artists' marketplace by copying the artwork and putting it onto merchandise. The artists could have *licensed* those images for use on T-shirts.

Is this happy little family just a bunch of sinister pirates? Are they just copying? Or are they stealing?

Just Because It's Easy Doesn't Mean It's Right

A key part of the problem is a tendency in the public mind to regard anything online as "information" and to regard that "information" as something that should be freely accessible. The news media, the lawmakers, and the technocrats have used the word *information* to represent everything that is digital, totally ignoring the connotations that reside in the word *information*. Every day we hear the terms *information age, information access,* and even *freedom of information.* And these catch phrases stick in people's minds without much critical thinking about what lies behind them.

There are certain assumptions that everyday people attach to the word *information.* Such as: it is just facts, lists, statistics, compilations of times or places, tables of chemical elements, and so forth. The word *information* has an anonymity to it. Information is just "out there." It exists. It was not crafted by a living, breathing, hardworking person. Information doesn't seem to equate in people's minds to being *product*—with all the corollary investment of labor and equipment used in its production.

But is art information? Is a movie information? Is a recording of music information? There is, certainly, information in each of these things. But these things are not information, pure and simple.

Art Is Not Information

Sure, there is information in art. But art is information exquisitely transformed. Art is information about form, color, line, composition, rhythm, but distilled in the soul of the artist. Artists use process to alter raw materials and the end result is fixed. Artists are the ultimate materialists. And, though there are those who will dispute it, even "pure" digital art is fixed in the form of 1s and 0s. These are not just random lists of 1s and 0s, utilitarian data as in phone book listings. They are the ineffable, coded, cherished formulas of flesh and blood artists, physical manifestations of years of training, experience, and creative expression, plus plain hard work. Art is more than information and, thus, it is more precious. Anybody who lumps artworks into the category of information dismisses the creator—the artist.

"Information Wants to Be Free"

The notion that "information wants to be free" was first advanced in a book called *The Media Lab,* written in 1987 by media pioneer Stewart Brand (founder of *The Whole Earth Catalog*, the Hacker's Conference, and a pioneering online community called the WELL).

Interestingly enough, Brand's very next sentence, following the statement "Information wants to be free," was the sentence, "Information also wants to be expensive." These two sentences were the lead-ins to an essay in which Brand explored the many complex issues around intellectual property: the copying of software, digital sampling of music, and so on.

When Brand wrote that "information wants to be free" he was not being glib, and the issues he analyzed were anything but trivial. He analyzed, for instance, the copyability of software (another variety of intellectual property), noting that in many cases being widely pirated has actually *enhanced* the popularity of a software product, assisting a popular product to spread even more rapidly than it otherwise would and consequently to become a standard. When software manufacturers were forced by non-copy-protected competitors to drop copy protection in 1986 and 1987, they discovered that what they lost in copyright protection they gained in ease of use and marketability of their products. Brand observed that software producers learned that they were selling a "relationship" with the consumer, not just the product.

In his essay, Brand went on to review the issues of sampling in the music industry and VCR piracy in the movie industry. The music industry supposedly has methods of payment in place in its BMI and ASCAP organizations. Royalties are supposed to be paid to performers each time the music is played. But it's not that simple. With the advent of digital sampling, bits and pieces of music are being used like auditory collage, a practice that challenges the whole system of remuneration to musicians. In the movie industry, lines of distribution ensure payment for viewing films. But wholesale copying of VCRs means that millions of dollars are "lost" in the process. Both of these industries face copyright conundrums. Brand discussed the idea that each new kind of information provider has to get used to the idea of "leakage" of intellectual property.

In analyzing methods of payment for creators of intellectual property, Brand was nothing if not thorough, exploring such concepts as pay-per-hit, subscription billing for electronic publishing, and selling the "relationship" with the end user. He made the case for the reliability of the *source* of information as opposed to the intrinsic quality of the information itself. He concluded that people will pay for a reliable source of information—as in a subscription to a magazine—and projected this concept into the digital era with the suggestion that this type of payment would work best for many forms of electronic publishing and communications.

The material that followed Brand's now-famous "information wants to be free" aphorism is thought provoking to owners of intellectual property. But his essay neglected one important thing: nowhere did he define the word *information.* Most crucially, he did not distinguish between information as raw data and information as creative product. That failure to make such a distinction, as well as the deliberate stylistic choice of metaphor—information personified as an entity with a life and a will of its own—was obviously a deliberate stylistic choice, intended to convey a notion of substantial value and subtlety.

Bitten By A Soundbite

Unfortunately, the misappropriation of the phrase "information wants to be free" by the sound-bite-gobbling public has been anything but subtle. On the tongues of those looking for a convenient excuse, it has become a convenient tag line for wholesale copying with its corollary potential for wholesale infringement.

When Brand anthropomorphised the word *information* he simultaneously depersonalized, or completely ignored, the creator of the information. It's as though information were just "out there." And information—in the form of facts, dates, chronologies, and so on—*is* just "out there." But art is not mere information.

By attributing personality and will to a thing called information, you imply that information has its own motivations and needs. As if information were in charge of its own dissemination, not people. As if information were out of control, not people. As if information, not people, could move about with free will.

Information does not want anything. It is something. People want. Information just sits there. Dumb. I believe that many of those who say that "information wants to be free" really mean, "I want free information." And while it's one thing to want the information contained in the phone book, it is an entirely different thing to want the information contained in art.

For that matter, there are other forms of "information" that people want, but that are substantively different from raw data, lists, or phone numbers. Does your

ON THE OTHER HAND...

Well, sure, technically—art, movies, music—it's just bits. Just 1s and 0s. But, hey, it's a whole lot more than that. If anything, it's alchemy. And precious alchemy, at that. Not to mention—it costs a small fortune to become an artist. School. Equipment. Starving 'til you get recognition. And they want to call that "information"? And they say my art is "information"? That it wants to be free? ☞

medical record want to be free? Your credit rating? Your unlisted phone number? Does your confidential employment information want to be free? A person may desire them to be so, for whatever purposes. But somehow the gleaning of information, all information, carries with it a sinister overtone. Someone takes your medical information. Why? For what purposes? Your credit card information. What for? Your employee reviews. Why?

For information to be free requires an actor to make it so. A human being must tap into information, must move it about, else it remains stuck in the aether. Information has no wants nor desires. People want.

When you assume that information wants to be free, you also, conveniently, shift responsibility for the movement of information onto the information itself and off of the shoulders of those who are, in fact, moving it around. That is why the line "information wants to be free" is so appealing to those who would like to see copyright die a digital death. They can claim that the information itself—your personnel records, your medical records, your credit card numbers, your artwork—*wants* to be copied and used. Then they can abdicate responsibility for having had anything to do with it.

Suddenly we have this medium—the Net—from which it is so very easy to copy. And the distance from appropriate copying to actual stealing is only a few small steps. Selling it as your own. Why not? After all, it's just information, right? It just wants to be free! Nobody's going to care. They'll never catch me. In the mind of a person without much moral grit, the line "information wants to be free" is all the excuse needed to rationalize what, in an analog world, would be stealing, plain, and simple. There lies the power of the sound bite taken out of context. It can lead to actions that are unrelated to the author's original content.

Returning to Common Sense

Now, just because it's the digital era doesn't mean we can't apply a little common sense to this thing, this copyright law. And, conversely, just because it's the digital era doesn't mean we get to toss out traditional behavioral precepts that have served personkind over the millennia. Ideas like the one that posits: "don't steal stuff" are pretty careworn at this point in time. But they persist. Reason is, they work. It's just that in the digital era, stealing can become depersonalized. To counter the tendency for our ethics to become "digitized," the best thing is to remember the simple fact that every piece of visual imagery we see on the Net, including QuickTime movies, films, videos, icons, cartoons, goofy graphics, photographs, snapshots, paintings, drawings—the entire cornucopia of fixed creative products—was created by real, live artists. It is not just anonymous bits. At the very least, common courtesy demands that permission be asked to copy these works. And, legally, it may be a requirement.

By now, I hope, I am preaching to the converted.

Ethics in Support of Copyrights

So you have finally come round to the economics of promoting your work online with free samples, and someone takes you at your word and takes one of your images. Problematic, this. Yes, it certainly feels awful when you see a portion of your work in another "artist's" collage. Used without your permission. Lifted from your own home page on the Web, no less. Why can't they just come up with their own images? And take their gleeps off mine?

Scratching the Itch to Consume

Technology has aggravated our desire to consume. These days the desire is for information. Computers have seemingly made our desires easier to obtain. Human beings are more than ever driven by computers in a desire to possess, to access, to eat up, to inhabit, to stake out, to get. History is pockmarked by the desire to consume our world—land, fuel, timber, minerals, money. Now it is a desire to consume information—images, data, words, bits—in a sort of manifest destiny of the information age. But behind all of that "information" are the creators of the information. It's not just "out there" unless it truly is just facts, statistics, lists of the elements, and so on. Someone created it.

This latest eating disorder of the soul, this voracious appetite for information, bits, bytes, data, the digital dumpings of every one and every thing in the aether will not make one happier, nor smarter, nor stronger, nor leave one satisfied. Nor will it make one an artist.

This greed, combined with the ease with which digital images can be copied, can lead to abuses of fair use and de minimus doctrines. This greed, combined with the sweet moral elixir of "information wants to be free" can lead to wholesale copyright infringements. Hey it's just a parody, man! Hey I just used a tiny piece of your art. No sweat. Hey, dude, it's just information and it wants to be free! And we usher in the fad of digital art in the form of montage and collage. Appropriation and misappropriation.

But consider this: information overload, in art, is the triumph of form over substance. Too much raw visual information is incomprehensible. Copying too much information in a frenzy of artistic consumerism leads to nothing but regurgitation. Wave upon wave of images, sounds, permutations, juxtapositions, variations on a rat's nest. Downloading twenty-five images from the Web and mixing them up in a stew of Photoshop filters does not make you a collage artist. Art is about selection. In order to harness information into a comprehensible form we must combine creativity, plus insight, plus experience, plus mind. Information alone is cold and brute and hulking. And aesthetically, when piled megabyte upon megabyte, it is ugly. This latest fad in digital art is no more than the cramming of as many images and techniques as possible into one art space, and it grows out of greed and expedience. Not from aesthetic vision.

What, you are asking, does this have to do with copyright law? Has she gone mad? It has this to do with copyright law.

There would not be so much heated debate about what is and what is not allowed under fair use and de minimis doctrines if artists were creating original works of art. Period. The way to turn down the heat on copyright infringement is to start doing original work. Stop using anyone's images except your own. If you want to do collage and photomontage, create all of your own elements for these works. Dispense, once and for all, with the notion that information wants to be free.

Ethics: Plain, Simple, and Informed

If copyrights are to work at all in the digital era, ethical consideration will have to be woven into the fabric of the Internet. People will have to learn not to copy artwork just because it is easy to do so. Not to pass off copied artwork as their own. Not to sell (steal) copied artworks just because it is easy. Or because it's unlikely that one will get caught. And that's the hardest concept of all. People will have to make ethical choices, plain and simple.

With each technological development in history has come a reexamination of fundamental human questions. Who am I? Why am I here? What is my purpose? How should I behave? What is good? What is bad? Social upheavals are the expected corollaries to technological change. The printing press. The automobile. The assembly line. At each of these technological junctures, people have dusted off ethics and reexamined age-old human assumptions about behavior. It's happening again, now, on the byways of the electronic superhighway. With this latest technological advance, the philosophers, professional and armchair, sit down again and debate, anew, whether simple truths can ever again be self-evident given the new technological wonders.

So let's roll up our sleeves, plop down on our armchairs for a moment, and consider the ethics of copying along the electronic superhighway.

Before people can make ethical choices, they need to be taught how to think critically. Currently most of the "education" about copyrights centers on review of copyright laws. That the discussion of copyrights on the Net contains only secondary references to the ethics of copying for personal use versus copying to steal, points, I believe, to a disturbing poverty of ethics in this digital age. That it sounds quaint for me to suggest that it is not ethical to copy another person's original creative output for any reasons other than personal enjoyment, further emphasizes this sorry lack.

At the close of an article in which he strongly questioned the future of copyrights online—"The Economy of Ideas: A Framework for Rethinking Patents and Copyrights in the Digital Age (Everything You Know about Intellectual Property Is Wrong)," *Wired* magazine, March 1994— John Perry Barlow gave a conspicuous nod to the importance of online ethics.

Barlow stated that he comes from the kind of small town where residents do not need to lock their doors because the ethics of the community are in good enough shape so as to prevail over burglars. Whether or not you agree with Barlow on the viability of copyright law, his point that communities with solid ethical standards work better and don't have to lean as hard on legal standards is true enough. Yet it begs the core issue of what really needs to be done to keep those ethical standards alive and kicking. Education is required. And that's hard. It requires teaching people about the difference between making a copy for private enjoyment and making a copy that leads to copyright infringement. It requires that we exercise a little common sense and teach a little critical thinking. That we closely examine the significance of sound bites such as "information wants to be free."

In her book *Who Owns Information*, Anne Wells Branscomb observed:

> *While there are three traditional sources of protection of property rights—ethics, technology, and law—the* **new electronic imagers may have to rely primarily upon creating an ethical environment in which their labors are appreciated and compensated accordingly....** *The law always lags behind technological advances and cannot, in any event, precede a consensus based upon ethical concepts the community is willing to support and sanction." (my emphasis)*

So where are we, here? Technology has presented us with the computer, a box with a brain. But it's a Pandora's box that can sometimes complicate and obfuscate simple human truths. Perhaps, as with other technologies that have threatened fundamental beliefs, it will precipitate a dusting off of old ideas, old theories of human behavior. And, like museum artifacts, those once familiar objects will reveal the usefulness beneath their fading forms.

FOR WHAT IT's WORTH...

Ethics in an Age of Technology: The Gifford Lectures, Volume Two
By Ian Barbour
HarperCollins Publishers
10 E. 53rd Street
New York, NY 10022
800/242-7737
ISBN 0-06-060934-6

A compilation of lectures that range across ethical issues in the technological era. Although the subjects covered are way beyond the scope of this book, it does present troubling ethical conundrums for our digital era. A good, meaty, if difficult, read.

The Media Lab: Inventing the Future at MIT
By Stewart Brand
Viking Books
Penguin USA
375 Hudson Street
New York, NY 10014
ISBN 0-670-81442-3

A late-1980s look at MIT's cutting-edge Media Lab, where many of today's concepts of on-line, hyperlinked, multimedia information were already being explored a decade ago.

Who Owns Information?
By Anne Wells Branscomb
Basic Books—A Division of HarperCollins Publishers, Inc.
10 E. 53rd Street
New York, NY 10022-5299
ISBN 0-465-09175-X

This is an intriguing, sometimes scary, book. It explores the flow of information in the digital era and discusses who has access to what and what you should know about it. It contains considerable discussion about ethical behavior and privacy issues.

AFTERWORD

Falling from This Wire Means Certain Death

Halfway though this book, I desperately needed a break. So I drove down to our local Farmer's Market one Sunday morning. It was a cloudy, cold Spring day. A big crowd was forming in one corner of the grounds and they were intermittently applauding and raising their voices in gasping "Ooooooh's" and "Ahhhhh's." I wandered over to see what was happening.

There in the center of the parking lot was stretched a tightrope. An exotically pretty young girl stood to one side. Her costume consisted of a leotard and tights, ballet slippers, and a variety of black scarves fastened at her

ON THE OTHER HAND...

Any Luddites out there? So who says we need to be part of the great Third Wave? Technology schmechnology! Who needs it anyway? It's just a pain. It makes my life more complicated than I ever dreamed possible. I don't have the time. We're all just sitting out here on our rumps, staring slack jawed into our screens. It's time to go outside. Take a hike. Dig in the garden. Or get back into our studios. That's the thing. We're artists, after all. Time to get back into the studio. Smell the turpentine. Get the hands dirty. Just because it's there, doesn't mean we have to use it. Who needs the electronic superhighway, anyway? Mile upon mile of wire and cable connecting billions of gleaming little computer terminals. I can't take it anymore! 🐂

waistline. Her very long black hair was raised into a high ponytail at the top of her head. Beneath the tightrope was a thin man wearing buccaneer leather boots, playing an electric fiddle in a minor key. As he played his fiddle, he swooped around on the ground under the tightrope, like a skater. And, most stunning of all, visually, was his five feet of hair which waved and flew and slithered around his burgundy velvet jacket as he moved.

The girl reached for the ladder and swung gracefully up to the tiny platform at one end of the tightrope. With a gesture we could feel as much as see, her face, her mind, her entire being completely transfigured themselves into an expression of trancelike concentration. She walked onto the tightrope. Below swirled her partner, decorating each of her moves with exquisite sounds from his violin and elegant swoops of his snaking hair. The girl stood in the center of the tightrope, then raised one of her legs completely over her head, doing the splits vertically. The crowd gasped and then was silent as the girl slowly, gracefully, lowered her leg, with meticulous attention to detail and form. She then slid her feet in opposite directions along the tightrope and did the splits again, this time horizontally on the length of the tightrope. Then she inched her feet back along the tightrope, defying common sense and gravity, until she stood upright again. The crowd was mesmerized. I was mesmerized

For the next eternity the girl and her partner performed enchanted variations on the theme of balance and grace, music and magic. Touchingly deft, horrifyingly dangerous, and magnificent under the clouded Spring sky.

Then the performance was over and we, the stunned audience, were mute. I walked away trembling, my heart thumping. Yet, wondering why. Then it came to me. I had just experienced art in real time, had been moved by the intensity of art performed in the moment. It was tangibly affecting. And completely alive and different from anything I had experienced in digital realms. Its intensity resided in the simultaneity of elegance and danger.

Anyone who has strolled through a museum and looked at paintings can tell you the simple truth that the same pictures viewed on a cathode ray tube are different. No doubt about it. The circus performers were so stunning that Spring day for the same reason. Art in real time is capable of physically affecting the human mind, spirit, and body.

Viewing artworks on the electronic superhighway is a powerful experience of a different kind. Working with digital images has its own special lure to the artist. Lacking the immediacy of art in real time, the electronic superhighway provides the artist with the impact of art in kaleidoscopic abundance. Artists need both—the depth of real-time experience and the breadth of cyber-space. The impact of the image as object and the impact of the image as idea. Going to the museum satisfies the first need: to let the eyeballs touch the object. Going net-surfing satisfies the second: to let the creative mind caress the concept. Nowhere is there greater potential for the immediate gratification of the artist's need to "see" than on the World Wide Web. For the first time in history, artists can skim the entire contents of the world's great museums in just minutes. The inspiration derived from such an experience is, in its own way, as breath-taking as the high wire act. What I realized that spring day was the value and significance of both types of experience—one real, one digital—in the life of an artist.

1995

The Virtual Gallery of the Louvre. A student has set up a Mac and a mouse and sits in front of a cathode ray tube, magic carpet style. Her pristine black workstation belies the radiant fervor of her creativity. An admiring circle of visitors nod and whisper among themselves, feeling both excited at being able to visit this talented student's loft and reluctant to break the spell of the Web. The student acts as tour guide, clicking deftly from Mondrian to Picasso to Cezanne. As image replaces image and the rich RGB color saturates the eyes of the beholders, the student picks up the pace. Clicking first to Renaissance grandeur. Then, clicking to medieval icons. Click, to the gaudy expressionists. Then click to bronzes. Click to clay. Click, to Ormolu. Click, Le Brun. Click, Klee. Click to Artemisia Gentileschi, Dalí, Rothenberg, Graves, Lichtenstein. Warhol and Kandinsky and Rego and Arp. Click and click and click again. Then one last click and back to black.

Flushed and bleary eyed, the viewers disband for sodas. But the student sits in front of her now dark screen, mesmerized, inspired. The world of artistic output has just flown before her eyes.

While her visitors mingle and joke, she starts a doodle on a notepad. Inspired, she sketches, then scans her little image into her computer. Then she opens it in a her new 3-D rendering program and is lost to her guests for three hours of intense transformative concentration. And while her mind's eye carries the impressions beamed from the virtual Louvre, she drifts in her own directions. Inspired, but not envious. Creative, but not acquisitive. In a pure flight of imagination, she works on her image, using the digital tools of this era. Born from a virtual cornucopia of the world's greatest art comes yet another art form, new and unique. Digital and spectacular. A distillation of this artist's experience and psyche. First 1's and 0's. Now raster lines. Now a color proof. Now an artist's proof. Now under glass. Signed: Circle C The Artist.

FREQUENTLY ASKED QUESTIONS ABOUT COPYRIGHT

1. Is there such a thing as innocent infringement? If I did not know I was infringing someone's copyright, I wouldn't be guilty of infringing, right?

> Wrong. Even if you were completely unaware of copyright law and made an infringing copy, you would still be an infringer if the case were brought to court, but you might find that the damages you had to pay would be less than if you were a *wilfull* infringer: one who knew what she was doing and did it anyway.

2. Do I need to obtain permission and pay license fees for every image I copy for a multimedia production?

> Yes, unless the images are in the public domain or are included in any of the other exceptions to copyrighted material. *When in doubt, a bell should go off: call an attorney for advice or do some serious, objective research before you copy.* Even if you intend to use your multimedia production in a private setting, such as in the privacy of your client's boardroom, you must contact the owner or controller of the copyright in each and every copyrighted segment that you want to use in your production. This includes visual elements as well as text, music, or sound. Contact the creators *before* you start your production, because obtaining permissions and clearances often takes a lot more time than you think it ought to. Do not assume they will necessarily be flattered to be in your production and that their permission is a given. You must also track down the ownership of images you may feel to be in the public domain, such as Renaissance paintings or ancient artwork, for instance. This is because the institution

that owns these works may have copyrights in the reproductions of them. Even though Tutankhamen's face is in
the public domain, individual photographs of this famous
face are copyrighted by the photographers who took them.

3. Do I need to transfer rights for usage of my images in writing?

Yes. Although oral agreements are binding, they can be
incredibly, frustratingly, expensively difficult to prove.
Any transfer of rights to copy, in the form of licenses,
should be done in writing. That way, you will be able to
state clearly how and where the licensee can use your
images *and* the licensee won't have to remember the
terms of your agreement. Sometimes a simple letter
agreement is enough. Sometimes more detailed, specific
terms are necessary, as in the case of multiple uses by a
corporate client.

4. Do I need to register my work with the Copyright Office to receive copyright protection?

No. But you will be in a better position if you have registered your work before the infringement occurs. For
instance, if you have registered before the infringement,
you can sue to collect attorney's fees.

5. How do I register my work?

Ask the United States Copyright Office for a copy of Form
VA (for works of Visual Arts; get it? Text applications are
filed on Form TX, audiovisual applications on Form PA).
Complete the form (it's a very simple one, with instructions
attached) and enclose the required printed copies (color
prints, transparencies, and so on) of your artwork. You may
also register a group of works on one form. Then send the
form, the copies of your images, and a $20 fee to: Register
of Copyrights, Copyright Office, Library of Congress,
Washington, DC 20559. Call the Forms Hotline for registration forms: 202/707-9100. Copyright registration goes
into effect on the date that the form, the copies of the
images, and the fee are received by the Copyright Office,
regardless of how long it takes for them to get back to you.

6. **May I use any person's name or snapshot in my work?**

> Sometimes yes, sometimes no. In general, if you're using an image for sales or promotional purposes, you can't. If you're using it for editorial illustration of the content of a work, you may be able to. But it's always safest to ask for permission, and most cautious publishers or distributors will insist on it. If it turns out that you need permission and you don't have it, prepare for a major claim against you based on invasion of privacy or appropriation of publicity rights.

7. **I've heard that I can use the images of famous people such as actors and politicians without getting their permission. Can I?**

> Famous people have a right to control commercial uses of their famous faces (and figures, in the case of Demi Moore and Sharon Stone and Sylvester Stallone). You might be able to use an image to illustrate in an editorial way, but the risks of being expensively wrong are so great that you really ought to check this one out with a lawyer. Even a cartoon parody of a famous person, when used in a commercial, resulted in a successful lawsuit. And there's no such thing as "fair use" in this context.

> Politicians are usually fair game—you don't need their permission to use their name or image in a work of art, but you might well if the image appears to endorse a product.

8. **As an advertising agency art director, may I use images—from artists' or photographers' promotional CDs for instance, or from the previously published work of an artist—for use in comprehensive layouts?**

> Strictly speaking, no. It is an infringement of the copyrights of the photographers or illustrators whose work you scan for use in your comp.

9. **What if my client asks me to scan or download the work of another artist or photographer in the creation of my artwork?**

   This frequently happens. You should diplomatically remind the client that this is a potential copyright infringement. But sometimes a client will insist. To protect yourself in such a situation, you could ask the client to obtain permission. And you should have an "indemnification clause" in your contract that would hold you harmless in such a situation if the artist makes a claim against you. And remember this: even if the client ordered you to infringe, you're still one of the infringers.

10. **Where can I get more information about copyright?**

    Ask for a free Copyright Information Kit from the Copyright Office, Information and Publications Section, Library of Congress, Washington, DC 20559. Or call the Public Information Office at: 202/707-3000. The Copyright Office publishes a lot of useful material, most of it free.

11. **May I scan in wrapping paper or marble paper to use as textures in my digital artworks?**

    It seems such an innocent thing to scan a bit of wrapping paper. But these paper designs are copyrighted, so you must obtain permission to use them. You may have to pay a fee for the license to use them.

12. **Should I put the ©, my name, and the year of creation on my work on the net?**

    OK. Let's assume you're going on-line with your own home page. You work up images and text and you send it "out there." Yes, do put the standard copyright notification on your work. And come up with another, more creative message to the effect that copying these works will be considered by you, the creator, to be an infringement. But do this with your eyes and mind open. Do not be so blithe as to assume nobody will download or copy your images. Conversely, consider easing up on the strict enforcement of your copyrights on-line. If you do, include a limited license that says, "Go ahead and use my work for your own noncommercial purposes, but not if you sell the product in which you use it."

13. What kinds of images may I use in my digital photomontages or illustrations? And who owns the copyright to my photomontage or multimedia production that contains other artists' works?

The best images to use are your own images. Take your own photographs. Compose your own images in a bit-mapped or vector drawing program. Use or alter the many thousands of clip-art and royalty-free images that are available free of licensing fees. When you use your own images, you are certain that you own the copyrights to them. If you use parts of images, or even whole images, of another artist or photographer, you must ask the creator for a license to do so. If the artist grants you a license, then you may use those images in your photomontages, digital illustrations, or multimedia works. As the creator of the photomontage or multimedia work, you will then own the copyright to that work as a whole, but not to the elements that belong to others. They still own their copyrights.

14. If I work on staff for someone, and my job description covers creative work, is there any way I can still own the copyrights to my creative output?

That work is work made for hire, and the copyright belongs to your employer. Only if you have a written contract that so states will you own the copyrights. But consider this: work you do while moonlighting, or that isn't a part of your duties, is *not* work made for hire; you own the copyright until you license it to someone else. So if you're a technical artist, and the boss asks you to do this year's Holiday Greeting Card design over the weekend, the design isn't work made for hire, and you own the copyright.

15. May I download and use in my work images I find on the Web?

No. While it's easy to do, it's pretty much certainly also easy infringement. No matter how distant the source of those images, someone probably owns the copyrights to them. Do not do this.

16. It's being rumored that some giant corporations are buying up copyrights for existing illustration and photography that was previously sold as "buyouts" to other corporations. The fear is that these corporate "raiders" will then market the images on CD-ROM, selling them as files of royalty-free images. Is this true?

As of this writing, there have been several rumors to this effect, all of which have been denied by the corporations alleged to be doing this. But it would be prudent for artists and their representatives to curtail buyouts on all artworks for all clients. At the very least, an artist should limit usage of the images and put the usage agreement in writing. Do not sign purchase orders with buyout language in them.

17. Yes, but what if I need the money? I don't have the clout as an artist to cross out terms on a company's standard agreement forms.

This is a problem for artists of every level. Frequently the plum corporate jobs come with a very high price. The artist has to sign a work-for-hire agreement or, what, for rights purposes, amounts to one in the form of a complete buyout of the usage of the image(s) for "any known media, now or to be developed in the future, anywhere in the universe." And if you think this is hyperbole, just read a few of the latest contracts out there. Another current strategy that clients use to secure copyrights to an artist's work is the old "issue-the-PO-midway-through-the-project" ploy. You're just about done with the project and along comes a purchase order with copyright buyout terms. Do not succumb to this tactic. Cross out and initial the offending terms. Granted, this is a difficult stand to take with a prestigious client, but artists must be willing to fight for their copyrights. This is a case where artists must band together to make their voices heard in the market-place. Insist on straight fees for specific usages and retain all other copyrights in your images. Take a pass on the projects that do not allow this. Or at least surrender with full and bitter knowledge of what you're doing. And spread the word about that client's pernicious business practices.

18. How about fractals? Can I use the formula for a fractal and the same color combinations as another fractal artist? Or is there copyright infringement in this?

Creating fractals from mathematical formulas does not infringe on anybody's copyrights. Generic mathematical formulas, based on random applications of numbers, can not be copyrighted. This is not to say that *all* formulas are not copyrightable. Some may well be, especially if they are based on proprietary methodologies. If you work with fractals and color them in the same manner as another fractal artist, this could be considered to be an infringement. It's like using a similar tool to produce a copied image. If you are aware of a particular execution of a fractal, then try to come up with your own version of it rather than copy it.

19. What kinds of materials are in the public domain?

Ideas, facts, words, names, slogans and short phrases (unless they are protected by trademark or service mark, trade secret, or unfair competition), blank forms, federal government works, formerly copyrighted works whose copyrights have expired, and works that have not been copyrighted. For more detailed information about things you may copy, see Chapter 3.

TO-DO LIST FOR ARTISTS

1. Evaluate your risk aversion level.

Before you go on-line, open your own home page on the World Wide Web, or put your work on CD-ROM, diskette, or any other form of digital file, consider your risk-aversion level. Ask yourself how you would feel if your images were pirated from any of these media. Are you very fearful of losing control of your copyrights? A little fearful? Or not at all concerned? If you are very fearful of losing control of your copyrights, do not put your work on the Net. If you are not at all concerned, then dive right into the traffic. If you come out somewhere in between, consider taking one small step at a time. For instance, put a few images onto CD-ROM as a kind of miniportfolio; put your circle "c" on the work and distribute this miniportfolio to a select few of your best clients or prospects. Keep a log of who has a copy of your CD, then sit back and watch. The thing with a risk-aversion level is that it may change as you gain confidence in the digital era. Reevaluate your attitudes about your copyrights from time to time.

2. Know the fundamentals of copyright law.

Put a bookmark in Chapters 2 and 3. Each time you review a contract or make a sale of an original work of art, scan through the basics of the law. Make sure you understand the terms of each sale and check out the wording on contracts to make sure your copyrights are adequately honored. Every time you make a conscious effort to review copyright basics, you'll reinforce your understanding of the laws. I also recommend that you send for Circular 92, *Copyright Law of the United States of America*, and that you purchase at least one of the very fine books on copyright laws written by attorneys (see Appendix D). Armed with these, you will be able to research specific copyright questions as they come up or, better yet, anticipate them *before* they come up.

3. Try not to copy anybody else's images.

Let your talent and creativity work without the crutch of appropriation. Be an original. Take up the artists' mantle of stubborn independence. If you are just too much of an individual to copy even a small portion of another artist's work, you'll be rewarded with complete peace of mind about copyrights. Freedom from such worries will release your creative energies. It's easy to be original using the latest digital software. New programs come on the market every day. Digital cameras. 3-D imaging packages. Whizzy new paint programs. Doing it yourself has never been easier. Or more creative.

4. Experiment with royalty-free images.

If you are convinced that your artistic concepts rest on collage or montage, or if you are a multimedia producer who needs a wide range of visual materials, then tap into the vast resource of royalty-free image files. This market was once populated by just a few mediocre images. No more! Now there are literally tens of thousands of photo-graphic and illustrative images from which to select. And they are very inexpensive.

5. Always respect other artists' copyrights.

If you are working on a concept that absolutely requires the work of other artists or creators, then scrupulously observe their copyrights. Always ask for permission and obtain a license for use of their work before you use their images.

6. A warning bell should go off when you are about to make a copy.

Any time you scan or download an image, do a screen capture, or make a drawing from a piece of "scrap," a little warning bell should go off. Ask yourself these questions:

Could this be copyright infringement? Are you making a copy for your personal use? For commercial uses? When in doubt about whether it's okay to copy something, ask first. Call your local professional artist or graphic design association. Or get the advice of an attorney who knows about copyright.

7.   If you think an image is in the public domain, check it out first.

With the latest trend of corporations purchasing rights to old artworks, you must be careful. When in doubt, check it out. Remember, too, the case of King Tut. His image is in the public domain, but photographs and drawings of his image may be copyrighted by the photographers and artists who made them. You might need to get a license to use a photograph from the museum where he resides, or from the publisher of the book in which the image you want appears, or from the photographer who made the photograph you want to use.

8.   Be particularly careful of fair use.

Since the fair use doctrine is one of the murkiest areas of copyright law, proceed with caution. To be on the safe side, call your professional arts organization or an attorney to make sure your use falls under the provisions of the statute. Do not assume that your use is fair use, even if you include attribution to the other artist(s) in your work, or even if you believe you are creating a parody of another known work of art. Since the area of fair use is so tricky and contains many pitfalls, it is better to seek advice *before* assuming your particular usage falls under its purview.

9.   Reevaluate your use of images in comprehensive layouts.

If you are an advertising agency art director or graphic designer, stop using the images of artists and photographers in comprehensive layouts without first obtaining permission to do so, even if it means paying appropriate usage fees. Call the artist or artist's rep before you use that image. Many artists and reps are very flexible when you call them in advance of using an image. Many of them told me they would probably waive usage fees for comprehensives. But they are less likely to look kindly on your usage if they discover it by accident. While it has been a standard practice to use any image in a comprehensive layout without obtaining permission or paying use fees, the digital era is changing all this. Photographers and their representatives are particularly concerned about usage of their images in comprehensives. A phone call is all it takes—before you use the image.

10. Strongly enforce your copyrights in all contractual relationships.

If you are a commercial artist, you should always read all contracts and purchase orders thoroughly. Know and understand the terms, the usages you are licensing, and the payment you will receive. Protect your copyrights in all your contractual relationships. If you are a fine artist, put all sales agreements in writing and be sure to include explicit wording about copyrights in the images you sell. And watch out for gallery agreements that cover more than the sale of the original work. Dealers didn't get to be dealers by being generous with artists.

11. Avoid work-made-for-hire contracts.

Any contract that has the words *work made for hire* or their equivalent most likley means you give up your copyright—*all* of it—in the work you produce for that client. (Technically, work made for hire has to be specifically ordered or commissioned by the client, and both you and the client must sign the agreement. Also, only certain kinds of work can be work made for hire. But why argue about whether work is work made for hire? Insist—politely— that the contract reflect the deal you've made and the rights you're willing to sell.) As far as what you own and what you don't, any contract that states that you sell all your rights to the client is practically the same as a work-made-for-hire contract, even if it does not have the specific wording *work made for hire*. Avoid these contracts whenever possible. Sometimes you are allowed to cross out the section of a client's contract that contains work-for-hire provisions. But make sure that the person who authorizes you to cross out the work-for-hire provision has the authority to let you do that and insist that an authorized person initial the change for the client. Carefully read all purchase orders. Often POs contain work-for-hire provisions in the fine print. They sometimes come to you in the middle of a project, once you've already done a lot of the work. Under those circumstances, remove any work-for-hire wording from the PO.

12. Always affix the ©, your name, and the year of creation to your artworks.

Although your copyrights are in effect whether or not you put the copyright notice on your work, you will have a better position in a court of law if the notice is clearly in view.

13. Register your artworks with the Copyright Office.

The same holds true with registration of the copyright in your images—your copyrights are in effect whether or not you register your artworks, but you get some valuable additional legal rights if you've registered. The simplest method of registration is "batch" registration of groups of related artworks. Registration is worth the time and effort, if someone infringes your work.

14. Do go on-line. Explore the electronic superhighway.

The electronic superhighway is an exciting place for an artist. Put some of your works on the Net, but not all of your works, nor your most valuable works. The experience of going on-line is exciting and can be valuable in terms of exposure of your work to a potential vast market.

15. Navigate the Net with your eyes open.

You may not be able to enforce your copyrights on-line. Until technology catches up with hack-ology or until the ethics of the on-line community become stainless, you will have to relax your copyrights on the electronic super-highway. If you cannot bring yourself to do this, then do not put your work out there.

16. Thank your admirers. Shine on your detractors.

In the virtual art world: you are not as hugely talented as the former say you are. You are not as bad as the latter might claim. Take it all with a shrug of the shoulders and a healthy grain of salt.

17. Keep up-to-date with the latest technological locks for your work.

But do so realizing that for every lock there will be a lock-picker. If it can be coded, it can be cracked. Sure, go ahead and protect your artwork using the latest techno-logical means. Watermarks, read-only document files, encryption. But remember that there are people out there who consider your lock to be their destiny. They will access your work one way or another. And, as long as there are hardcopies of your work—in the form of pub-lished magazine illustrations, posters, greeting cards, and so on—there is always the possibility that someone will scan your work.

18. Give away free samples on-line.

Consider using the Net as an arena to promote your work and your reputation. Put samples out there, free of charge, free of copyrights. But remember: Information is cheap. Art is dear. Allow only a small portion of your art to exist as samples. You will probably attract at least a few buyers. Then ask for the full market value for your original works. Promote cheap, sell high.

19. Make some of your work into exclusive limited editions or "prints."

For instance: there are large-format Iris printers that can reproduce a digital file on 100 percent rag Arches paper up to 45 inches high. These elegant prints are a cross between a watercolor and a serigraph. Matted and framed, these handsome custom prints are a valuable high-ticket product for you to market. Sell these hand-crafted objects for the maximum amount the market will bear. With the abundance of images on billions of cathode-ray tubes of the future, human acquisitiveness—the desire for tactile experience, to hold, to touch, to own the precious object—will increase. In a virtual world, people will desire actual objects more than ever before.

20. Know your enemies.

Do not be concerned about the innocent infringers: the millions of moms and dads and kids who might download your images to look at or to make copies of for what's really just personal use. But do be concerned if someone out there takes your images and markets them. Worry about the serious commercial infringers, and, if you find out they are copying your work, go after them. But before you "go after" a serious infringer, ask yourself these questions: Is my market greatly damaged by this infringement? My reputation? My artwork? If, after considerable soul-searching, you want to pursue the infringer, then move fast but start conservatively. Call your local professional organization and ask its advice. Look into arts mediation and arbitration services. If you feel that your damages are extensive, call an attorney who specializes in copyright law.

21. Keep up with the latest technological developments for direct marketing of artworks on the net.

Very soon there will be virtual banks and secure telephone lines for selling goods on-line using credit cards. These developments will enhance your marketing efforts in the virtual world.

22. Start a copyright discussion group.

Contact your local professional art or lawyers for the arts organization. Start a copyright discussion group. Read some books. Get together with some friends and share the cost of an hour of lawyer's time for a little private seminar. Collect a portfolio of current and historic works of art that contain copied elements of other artists' works. Then look at those images analytically and discuss copyrights in terms of each individual work. By reviewing these images with other artists and attorneys you will gain a practical education in the fine art of copyrights.

23. Get involved in setting copyright policy.

Join a professional arts organization. Lobby. Picket. Write letters. Send e-mail. Sign petitions. Do something positive!

24. Stay informed.

Read anything and everything about copyrights on the electronic superhighway. It is a quicksilver field, with developments breaking daily. (I know you're too busy. But this is important.)

ORGANIZATIONS

Advertising Photographers of America
7201 Melrose Avenue
Los Angeles, CA 90046
800/272-6264

Allworth Press
10 E. 23rd Street, #400
New York, NY 10010
212/777-8395

Books of interest to artists: business, legal, and so on.

American Center for Design
233 E. Ontario, #500
Chicago, IL 60611
800/257-8657

A national association for graphic design professionals, this organization
sponsors exhibitions, publishes a newsletter, and is a resource center for
information on graphic design.

American Institute of Graphic Arts
164 Fifth Avenue
New York, NY 10010
212/807-1990

American Society of Media Photographers
14 Washington Road, #502
Princeton Junction, NJ 08550
609/799-8300

Association for Computing Machinery
1515 Broadway, 17th Floor
New York, NY 10036
212/869-7440

Sponsor of the annual Siggraph Conference, the ACM provides computer artists with the latest information on computer hardware and software and the latest in computer graphics research.

California Lawyers for the Arts (Los Angeles)
1549 11th Street, #200
Santa Monica, CA 90401
310/395-8893

California Lawyers for the Arts (Oakland)
247 4th Street, Suite 110
Oakland, CA 94607
510/444-6351

California Lawyers for the Arts (San Francisco)
Fort Mason Center, Building C, Room 255
San Francisco, CA 94123
415/775-7200

Computer Professionals for Social Responsibility (CPSR)
P.O. Box 717
Palo Alto, CA 94301
415/322-3778
E-mail: cpsr@cpsr.org

The mission of CPSR is to provide the public and policy makers with realistic assessments of the power, promise, and problems of information technology.

Conference on Computers, Freedom and Privacy
Hal Abelson, General Chair
Laboratory for Computer Science
Massachusetts Institute of Technology
Cambridge, MA 02139
E-mail: <cfp96@mit.edu>
WWW page: http://web.mit.edu/cfp96/

Established in 1991 to bring together experts in technology, law, computer science, business, public policy, law enforcement, and government and other interested parties to explore the effects of computer and telecommunications technology on freedom and privacy.

Electronic Frontier Foundation
1550 Bryant Street #725
San Francisco, CA 94103
415/668-7171
E-mail: ask@eff.org

Founded July 1990 to assure that the principles found in the Constitution and Bill of Rights are protected in the digital era.

Government Liaison Services, Inc.
3030 Clarendon Boulvard
Arlington, VA 22201
800/642 6564

This is one of many copyright search firms located in Arlington and Alexandria, Virginia; in Washington, D.C.; and in New York. I have personally used the services of this firm and found the staff to be prompt and very helpful.

Graphic Artists Guild
11 W. 20th Street, 8th Floor
New York, NY 10011
212/463-7730

KPFA-FM
Telecommunications Radio Project
1929 Martin Luther King Jr. Way
Berkeley, CA 94704
800/735-0230

Call for cassettes, transcripts, and resource sheets of "Communications Revolution" programs.

Lawyers for the Creative Arts
213 W. Institute Place, Suite 411
Chicago, IL 60610
312/944-2787

Free legal assistance for artists and arts organizations.

National Association of Desktop Publishers
462 Old Boston Street
Topsfield, MA 01983
800/874-4113

Publishes a monthly journal and a newsletter of interest to graphic designers and computer artists who do desktop design.

Professional Photographers of America, Inc.
57 Forsyth St. N.W., #1600
Atlanta, GA 30303
404/522-8600

An international association with the largest membership of professional image makers in the world.

SPAR
The Society of Photographers and Artists Representatives
60 E. 42nd Street, #1166
New York, NY 10165
212/779-7464

Stanford Law and Technology Policy Center
Stanford Law School
Crown Quadrangle
Stanford, CA 94305-8610
415/725-7788 (phone)
415/725-1861 (fax)
E-mail: Law.Tech.Policy@Forsythe.Stanford.edu

A nonpartisan, university-based research center dedicated to issues of technology, law, and policy.

Volunteer Lawyers for the Arts
1 E. 53rd Street
New York, NY 10022
212/319-2910 (hot line for artists)

This national organization publishes the VLA National Directory which lists dozens of VLA groups across the United States; $15. Call the hot line. The VLA also conducts conferences and seminars on current legal issues of interest to artists.

appendix d

FURTHER READINGS

Adobe Magazine (formerly Aldus Magazine)
Adobe Systems Inc.
411 First Avenue S.
Seattle, WA 98104-2817
206/628-2321

A great source of creative graphics and tips and tricks for graphic designers and artists.

ARTnews Magazine
ARTnews Subscription Service
P.O. Box 56590
Boulder, CO 80322-6590
800/284-4625

One of the best magazines covering the current fine-art scene. Not too precious for the average reader, yet meaty and informative for the professional fine or graphic artist.

Being Digital
By Nicholas Negroponte
Alfred A. Knopf, Inc.
201 E. 50th Street
New York, NY 10022
800/638-6460
ISBN 0-679-43919-6

A series of articles exploring the vast reaches of cyberspace. Written by one of the foremost thinkers of the digital era.

The Brothers Duchamp
By Pierre Cabanne
Little, Brown & Company
1271 Avenue of the Americas
New York, NY 10020
800/343-9204
ISBN 0-8212-0666-4

This is one of those wonderful big art books, with plenty of color pictures and a wealth of historical information about the unique vision of Marcel Duchamp, who may well have been the father of parody in the fine-art world.

Business and Legal Forms for Graphic Designers
By Tad Crawford and Eva Doman Bruck
Allworth Press
10 E. 23rd Street #400
New York, NY 10010
212/777-8395

California Painters: New Work
By Henry T. Hopkins and Jim McHugh
Chronicle Books
275 Fifth Street
San Francisco, CA 94103
800/722-6657
ISBN 0-87701-593-7

Copying in fine art continues right up to the most recent art movements. This book includes contemporary paintings with many "copied" or derivative elements from the works of other painters. Created by such diverse artists as Alexis Smith, Jess, and Rupert Garcia, these paintings demonstrate that copying, in one form or another, continues yet today. And, of course, these artworks demonstrate how public domain and fair use doctrines can work, legally, using copied materials.

A Canticle for Leibowitz

By Walter M. Miller, Jr.
Bantam Books
666 Fifth Avenue
New York, NY 10103
800/223-6834
ISBN 0-553-27381-7

What would happen if humanity had to start all over again without its technology? This intriguing science fiction novel explores human knowledge after an apparent atomic war. Engineering is kept alive by a band of somewhat comical and misinformed monks.

Communication Arts Magazine

P.O. Box 10300
410 Sherman Avenue
Palo Alto, CA 94303
(415) 326-6040

The sine qua non of graphic design magazines, CA always features the best in the field. Tad Crawford's regular column is a great source of copyright information.

Computer Artist Magazine

PennWell Publishing Company
1421 S. Sheridan
Tulsa, OK 74112
918/835-3161

A must if you are a computer illustrator. Cutting-edge ideas and tips. Learn all about encryption. An in-depth study about how and why to lock things in the digital age.

Computers, Pattern, Chaos & Beauty
By Clifford Pickover
St. Martin's Press, Inc.
175 Fifth Avenue
New York, NY 10010
800/221-7945)
ISBN 0-312-06179-X

If you are not familiar with Clifford Pickover's amazing computer graphics and intriguing theories, you are in for a treat. Lots of thought-starters and inspiration for digital artists.

The Computer Privacy Handbook
By Andre Bacard
Peachpit Press
2414 Sixth Street
Berkeley, CA 94710
510/548-4393
ISBN 1-56609-171-3

Everything you need to know about privacy in the digital era, including much about cryptography.

The Copyright Handbook: How to Protect and Use Written Works
By Stephen Fishman
Nolo Press
950 Parker Street
Berkeley, CA 94710-9867
800/992-6656
ISBN 0-87337-241-7

This book is for writers, but it is also an excellent resource for artists. The information is very detailed, but presented in a conversational manner. Copyright forms are in the back.

Copyright Law of the United States of America
Circular 92
United States Copyright Office
The Library of Congress
Washington, DC 20559
202/512-1800

A fairly small government document. Copyright law, chapter and verse. Not a great read, but a valuable reference for the professional artist.

Corel Magazine
Omray Inc.
9801 Anderson Mill Road, Suite 207
Austin, TX 78750
800/856-0062

Leading CorelDraw users contribute tips and tricks.

Dalí
By Robert Descharnes
Harry N. Abrams, Inc.
100 Fifth Avenue
New York, NY 10011
800/345-1359
ISBN 0-8109-0830-1

Dalí "copied" many famous artworks in the course of exploring his subconscious creative terrain. But, even in terms of today's copyright laws, his work would be judged to be acceptable under fair use. To discover why, take a good long look at some of the works included in this book.

"The Economy of Ideas: A Framework for Rethinking Patents and Copyrights in the Digital Age (Everything You Know about Intellectual Property Is Wrong)"
By John Perry Barlow
Wired Magazine, March 1994

This is a "must" for anyone interested in copyrights in the digital era. It is one of the most well-known arguments against copyrights and is well worth studying.

Ethics in an Age of Technology
By Ian Barbour
Harper San Francisco
HarperCollins Publishers
10 E. 53rd Street
New York, NY 10022
800/242-7737
ISBN 0-06-060935-4

Explores every aspect of ethical concern for the digital age. Reprints from the Gifford Lectures.

Graphic Artists Guild Handbook: Pricing & Ethical Guidelines, 8th Edition
Graphic Artists Guild
11 W. 20th Street
New York, NY 10011-3704
212/463-7730 (phone)
212/463-8779 (fax)

The first book an artist should purchase for information about copyrights, contracts, and pricing guidelines. The bible on these subjects, it is revised whenever industry standards change.

The Hacker Crackdown
By Bruce Sterling
Bantam Books
1540 Broadway
New York, NY 10036
800/223-6834
ISBN 0-553-56370-X

A fascinating look into the world of hackers and their defenders. Reveals the hysteria surrounding hacking, within the ranks of the general public and in the law enforcement community.

HOW Magazine
P.O. Box 5250
Harlan, IA 51593-0750
800/333-1115

An excellent magazine that features how-to articles for the graphic designer and commercial artist. From production tips to accounting to current copyright information, this magazine provides a lot of solid information.

Intellectual Property and the National Information Infrastructure: A Preliminary Draft of the Report of the Working Group on Intellectual Property Rights
Richard Maulsby
Director Office of Public Affairs
U.S. Department of Commerce
Patent and Trademark Office
Washington, DC 20231
703/305-8341

This document contains the Working Group's efforts to deal with copyrights in the digital era. While it is a preliminary draft, it contains an overview of the basic issues that Washington is grappling with and will give artists a flavor of the "official" government view. To obtain a copy, contact:

Intellectual Property in the Age of Electronic Information
Office of Technology Assessment
E-mail Linda Garcia at: lgarcia@ota.gov

An interesting and in-depth look at information in the digital era. Published the United States Congress, it is a good look at the myriad issues that face owners of intellectual property.

Internet World magazine
P.O. Box 713
Mt. Morris, IL 61054
800/573-3062

One of a fine group of new magazines dealing with issues on the Net.

Legal Guide for the Visual Artist
By Tad Crawford
Allworth Press
10 E. 23rd Street #400
New York, NY 10010
212/777-8395
ISBN 0-8015-4471-8

Tad Crawford writes about legal issues for artists and graphic designers. This book is a must for anyone in the business. Check out his regular monthly column in *Communication Arts* magazine, too.

Macworld Magazine
Subscription Services
P.O. Box 54529
Boulder, CO 80322-4529
800/288-6848

The source magazine for the latest hardware and software for Mac systems.

Magritte
By A. M. Hammacher
Harry N. Abrams, Inc.
100 Fifth Avenue
New York, NY 10011
800/345-1359
ISBN 0-8109-0278-8

The works of Magritte are filled with visual references to other artists' works and well worth studying in terms of today's fair use doctrine, which is discussed in more detail in Chapter 3.

Mazes for the Mind
By Clifford Pickover
St. Martin's Press, Inc.
175 Fifth Avenue
New York, NY 10010
800/221-7945
ISBN 0-312-08165-0

An inspiring book jammed with computer graphics and ideas. Fabulous and fantastical images, which may also be found on Mr. Pickover's WWW site listed in Appendix E.

The Media Lab: Inventing the Future at MIT
By Stewart Brand
Viking Books
Penguin USA
375 Hudson Street
New York, NY 10014
212/366-2000
ISBN 0-670-81442-3

An in-depth look at mid-1980s research at MIT. And home of the oft-quoted "information wants to be free."

Multimedia Law for Artists: A Handbook Supplementing the Multimedia Seminar
California Lawyers for the Arts
Fort Mason Center, Building C, Room 255
San Francisco, CA 94123
415/775-7200

Articles and information compiled by California Lawyers for the Arts for one of their many valuable seminar sessions. A good reference.

Multimedia Law Handbook
By J. Dianne Brinson and Mark F. Radcliffe
Ladera Press
3130 Alpine Road, Suite 200-9002
Menlo Park, CA 94025
800/523-3721
ISBN 0-96391-0-7

A detailed look at multimedia law. Well written and understandable with extensive exploration of fair use situations. Also includes useful form contracts, but be careful to adapt them to your situation.

Multimedia Magazine
Redgate Communications Corp.
660 Beachland Blvd.
Vero Beach, FL 32963
407/231-6904

If you are working in multimedia, this publication will help guide the way. Excellent for computer artists in other fields, too.

.net Magazine
Future Publishing Ltd.
Somerton
Somerset, England TA11 6TB

A British publication, it has a slightly different slant on the Net. Written with that usual British wit and intelligence.

OnLine Design Magazine
2261 Market Street, #331
San Francisco, CA 94114
415/334-3800

Cutting edge graphics and much solid information.

PC Magazine
P.O. Box 54093
Boulder, CO 80322-4093
800/289-0429

The source magazine for the latest hardware and software for PC systems.

Pop Art: A Continuing History
By Marco Livingstone
Harry N. Abrams, Inc.
100 Fifth Avenue
New York, NY 10011
800/345-1359
ISBN 0-8109-3770-77

A *big* book, absolutely loaded with Pop images and almost every page contains artworks with some form of copying in them—from logos to products to famous faces to previous artworks. The accompanying text tracks in detail the history of the Pop movement.

Publish Magazine
Subscriber Services
P.O. Box 5039
Brentwood, TN 37024
800/656-7495

This is *the* magazine for the computer graphic design and art professional. Focuses on a wide range of issues in the digital era, provides monthly in-depth analyses of industry issues—from business to production to copyrights.

Release 1.0
EDVenture Holdings, Inc.
104 Fifth Avenue, 20th Floor
New York, NY 10011
212/924-8800
$595 per year and worth every penny

This important monthly newsletter provides readers with Esther Dyson's unique take on the Net. She is one of the key thinkers of the era and well worth investing your hard-earned dollars and valuable time. Her views on making a living on the Net and corollary issues about intellectual property are important to the professional artist.

Secrets of a Super Hacker
By The Knightmare
Loompanics Unlimited
P.O. Box 1197
Port Townsend, WA 98368
206/385-5087
ISBN 1-55950-106-5

An excellent look into the world of the hacker. This book introduces the reader to the mind behind the hack, as well as to the tools of the trade.

The Studios of Paris: The Capital of Art in the Late Nineteenth Century
By John Milner
Yale University Press
302 Temple Street
New Haven, CT 06511
203/432-0960
ISBN 0-300-04749-5

A large paperback picture book that shows and describes the life of the artist in the late nineteenth-century Paris art scene. This book starts off by exploring the topic of student artists copying paintings in the Louvre and provides further insight into why these artists copied.

United States Court of Appeals for the Second Circuit, 91-7396.
Art Rogers, Plaintiff-Appellee-Cross-Appellant, against Jeff Koons and Sonnabend Gallery, Inc., Defendants-Appellants-Cross-Appellees
On appeal from the United States District Court for the Southern District of New York
July 22, 1991

The Virtual Community
By Howard Rheingold
Addison-Wesley Publishing Co.
One Jacob Way
Reading, MA 01867
617/944-3700
ISBN 0-201-60870-7

The first book you should read if you want to explore cyberspace. Written by one of the pioneering members of the WELL, it is filled with the information, people, ideas, and concepts of an on-line "virtual" community.

Who Owns Information?
By Anne Wells Branscomb
Basic Books
A Division of Harper Collins Publishers, Inc.
10 East 53rd Street
New York, NY 10022-5299
800/242-7737
ISBN 0-465-09175-X

This is an intriguing, sometimes scary, book. A look into the flow of information in the digital era. Who has access to what and what you should know about it. Considerable discussion about ethical behavior and privacy issues.

Wired Magazine
520 Third Street, 4th Floor
San Francisco, CA 94107
415/222-6200

Arch, avant garde, and sometimes off the deep end. But important reading for artists in the digital era.

The Writer's Legal Companion
By Brad Bunnin and Peter Beren
Addison-Wesley Publishing Co.
One Jacob Way
Reading, MA 01867
617/944-3700
ISBN 0-201-14409-3

a p p e n d i x   e

ON-LINE PLACES: MORE COPYRIGHT INFORMATION; AND ART ON THE WEB

More Copyright Information

The ads conference at the WELL
The advertising conference on the WELL is worth the membership if you are looking for a discussion forum on advertising. People in this conference are in the business and discuss the meaning of the Net, sometimes very heatedly, from a marketing perspective.

Copyright Information on the WWW
U.S. Patent and Trademark Office
http://www.uspto.gov/

The eff (Electronic Frontier Foundation) conference at the WELL
Hosted by founding members of the Electronic Frontier Foundation, this conference frequently ranges over copyrights in the digital era and much archived discussion is available on the topic. Sometimes there is more opinion than fact, but discussion is always thought provoking.

hannah_klein@hud.gov
This is the on-line government access to request information on copyrights (20 pages).

Topic 12 in the Byline conference at the WELL—ASJA Contract Watch
This interesting conference is for nonfiction writers. But many of the issues are parallel, especially relating to copyrights and contracts. A good resource with names of companies that have hidden work-for-hire clauses in their contracts.

Art on the World Wide Web

These Web sites show you how some artists and designers are making use of Web pages to promote and "sample" their work. Also included are places to sell your artwork on the Net. All of them are very effective, visually inspiring.

Artcellarx is a virtual art gallery where you can sell your work, browse others' work, and purchase artworks. All media.
http://www.artcellarex.com/ace/

Chickens on the Electronic Highway, a work-in-progress. Computer art, stories, weirdness, and paintings by Mary E. Carter.
http://www.well.com/user/themook

Laurie McCanna is a computer illustrator and type designer. She provides visitors to her site with free samples and a good overview of her portfolio.
http://www.mccannas.com

Clement Mok Designs' home page demonstrates excellent use of a Web site to promote a design firm.
http://www.cmdesigns.com

Clifford Pickover has the best job in the world. Resident artist for IBM. His Web site graphics are stunning!
http://sprott.physics.wisc.edu/pickover/home.htm

Web Museum. A great and ever-changing art exhibit. Excellent quality. Broad range of styles.
http://mistral.enst.fr/

Daniel Will-Harris is a graphic and type designer, writer, and computer graphics expert. A fun Web site.
http://www.will-harris.com/daniel/design.htm

SOFTWARE AND OTHER PRODUCTS

3DFAX

InfoImaging Technologies, Inc.

3977 East Bayshore Road

Palo Alto, CA 94303

415/960-0100 (phone)

415/960-0200 (fax)

E-mail: info@infoimaging.com

Adobe Acrobat

Adobe Systems

1585 Charleston Road

P.O. Box 7900

Mountain View, CA 94039

800/833-6687 or 415/961-4400

Portable-document software

Common Ground

No Hands Software

1301 Shoreway Road, #220

Belmont, CA 94002

800/598-3821 or 415/802-5800

Portable-document software

HoTMetaL Pro

Soft Quad

56 Aberfoyle, 5th Floor

Toronto, Canada M8X2W4

416/239-4801

Pretty Good Privacy
ViaCrypt
2104 W. Corea Avenue
Phoenix, AZ 85029
602/944-0773

Encryption software

Seymour/Online Image Resource
Picture Network International, Ltd.
2000 14th Street North
Arlington, VA 22201
800/764-7427

ROYALTY-FREE IMAGES

Image Club Graphics: By far one of the most exciting resources for royalty-free image collections is Image Club Graphics. If you are not on its catalog mailing list, you should be. The image collections it offers are of a consistently high quality and it changes and updates offerings frequently.

Most of the clip-art and photographic collections that Image Club offers are available royalty-free for use in advertising and graphic design. For the fine artist, there are one or two restrictions that would require a licensing fee. For instance, if you use a combination of clip art and photography to make a composition in a photo-manipulation program, then produce a limited edition of 200 archival prints for sale at a gallery, there would be a licensing fee required. But these fees are surprisingly low and restrictions are very limited. Just call first, if you have a usage question. The folks at Image Club are very friendly and helpful. Among the collections that I like the most are:

- **Digital Stock Corporation**: Twenty royalty-free volumes of gorgeous color photographs. Every image comes in five different file sizes. Photographers featured include: Mike Sedam (Western Scenics), Joshua Ets-Hokin (Food), and Robert Yin (Undersea Textures). Categories of photographs include Babies and Children; Business and Industry, Textures and Backgrounds, and Space and Space Flight. More than 2,000 images in all twenty volumes.

- **Neo Retro Volume 34**: A collection of 1950s cartoon images. Very hip, very of the era. Weird and wonderful. All black-and-white images, they can enhance your client's newsletters, ads, or T-shirts.

- **Photogear Backgrounds, Snackgrounds, and Fancy-fabrics**: Color photography of all kinds of textural backgrounds, from gorgeous marble to pretzels to silks and satins. Colorful, rich in detail, fun and imaginative. Textures you can use to enhance your photomontages and digital illustrations.

CMCD: The Visual Symbols collections, assembled by San Francisco designer Clement Mok, are photographs of things, reproduction quality, available unmasked. Each collection features 100 images of objects from birds' nests to rubber duckies, hands to boots, telephones to goldfish, up to and including visual "clichÈs" such as the glass half full/half empty.

Digital Wisdom Royalty-Free Body Shots: A photographic collection of 300 shots of people in all kinds of situations, full figure, torso, and group shots. Useful for advertising and also for fine artists who want to satirize contemporary life.

Image-A-Rama!: Includes 4,000 royalty-free images of people, places, things, buildings, flowers, street signs. The CD-ROM provides you with low-resolution images for selecting purposes, then you send for the high resolution versions for use in your work.

Cartesia MapArt: An excellent source of maps for graphic design. Includes world maps, continents, countries, states, and provinces. Also states of the United States with interstate highways, state highways, and counties. Fully editable in Illustrator, FreeHand, and CorelDraw.

AdArt: If you are a designer or advertising art director or if you are a fine artist and are creating parodies of images of contemporary society, here is a huge collection of logos, trademarks, and credit card art. All the brand name product logos, from McDonalds to Harley-Davidson and more.

Corel Professional Photos: Available on CD-ROM, this is a huge collection of thousands of royalty-free Kodak photographs. Corel provides an enormous listing of photos, and the price is remarkable at about $14 per CD. These are the middle-market images, not the most creative, but very useful for collage, multimedia, and graphic design.

Texture Magic: Contains 24-bit TIFF textures and special effects good for texture mapping, photomontaging, and multimedia backgrounds. Good colors and unusual effects.

Photo Graphic Edges: They say God is in the details, and this collection of 650 edge effects can really enhance any photograph or image. These edge patterns mimic darkroom techniques and can be combined for unique special effects.

Past-Tints Antique Illustrations: A fine collection of more than 300 antique art line illustrations. Animals, people, garden things, old-time transportation. Flowers, fruit, birds, and insects. Excellent for spots in brochures, hang-tag art, and some fine-art applications.

Planet Art: An excellent collection of classical art. Paintings by Botticelli, Hopper, Raphael, and Leonardo da Vinci, to name only a few. Graphics include European posters, antique maps, medieval alphabets and devices, Arabic tiles, French posters, William Morris patterns. Great!

Publisher's Task Force: I really like working with contemporary iconography, and the Task Force collections are great for those common icons of everyday life. Not "arty," but just the thing for montage, collage, and multimedia projects. The collections offer every possible image from the Capitol dome to baseball players, piggybanks to aircraft. Trucks, babies, tulips, cute kitties. Ready for your editorial comments!

Art Gallery: Now here's a trend to watch. Microsoft and some other corporate entities are purchasing some of the copyrights on art that is already in the public domain. Microsoft's Art Gallery gives you Britain's entire National Gallery painting collection, all 2,200 of them, for use, free, as screen backdrops or in company presentations, but not for use in a product that you then sell to someone else. A lovely collection to look at. Call for further information about royalty-free usages as they apply to your particular project.

These are just a few of the many hundreds of clip and photo art collections available to the artist, art director, or designer. By using royalty-free images in your original artwork, you assure yourself and your clients of no-hassle copyrights. And these gorgeous digital collections provide you with excellent quality images in standard file formats such as TIFF and EPS.

Cartesia
5 S. Main Street, Box 757
Lambertville, NJ 08530
800/334-4291

CMCD Library of Visual Symbols
600 Townsend Street, Penthouse
San Francisco, CA 94103
415/703-9900

Corel Professional Photos
Publishers's Toolbox
P.O. Box 620036
Middleton, WI 53562
800/348-8331

Dover Clip Art Series
Dover Publications, Inc.
Dept. 23
31 E. 2nd Street
Mineola, NY 11501
800/223-3130

Graphics Express Catalog
Graphics Express
One Datran Center, #1500
9100 S. Dadeland Boulevard
Miami, FL 33156
800/335-4054
- Globe Shots
- Body Shots
- Photographic Edges
- Texture Magic

Image-A-Rama
from PhotoDisc Inc.
2013 Fourth Avenue
Seattle, WA 98121
206/441-9355

Image Club Graphics Inc. Catalog
U.S. Catalog Fulfillment Center
c/o Publisher's Mail Service
10545 W. Donges Court
Milwaukee, WI 53224-9967
800/387-9193

Microsoft Art Gallery
Note to Mary:
Need address.
800/426-9400

Mountain High Maps
Digital Wisdom Inc.
P.O. Box 2070
Tappahannock, VA 22560
800/800-8560

Past-Tints Antique Illustrations
Periwinkel Software
7475 Brydon Rd.
La Verne, CA 91750
800/730-3556

Planet Art
Available through:
Publisher's Toolbox
P.O. Box 620036
Middleton, WI 53562
800/348-8331

Task Force
Available through:
Graphics Express
One Datran Center, #1500
9100 S. Dadeland Boulevard
Miami, FL 33156
800/335-4054

FAST PERMISSIONS: RESOURCES

The following organizations can help locate original artworks and obtain permission to use them fast. The people are very friendly and helpful and handle thousands of artists and their works.

Artists Rights Society (ARS)
65 Bleeker Street
New York, NY 10012
212/420-9160

This organization was able to help me track down artworks that had previously yielded only a dead-end from other sources. Very helpful. After obtaining permission to use the images, I then called the next resource to obtain transparencies for reproduction.

Art Resource
65 Bleeker Street, 9th Floor
New York, NY 10012
212/505-8700

Agence Photographique de la Reunion Des Musées Nationaux
10, Rue de L'Abbaye
75006 Paris, France
40 13 46 01 (fax)

Source for artworks from the Louvre.

appendix i

FIGURES

Figure 1: *L.H.O.O.Q*, Marcel Duchamp

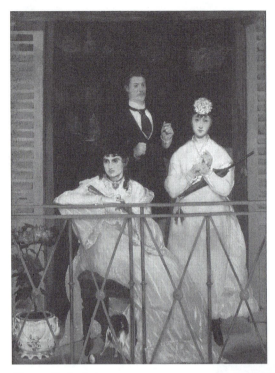

Figure 2: *Le Balcon*,
Edouard Manet

Figure 3: *Perspective II: Manet's
Balcony*, Rene Magritte

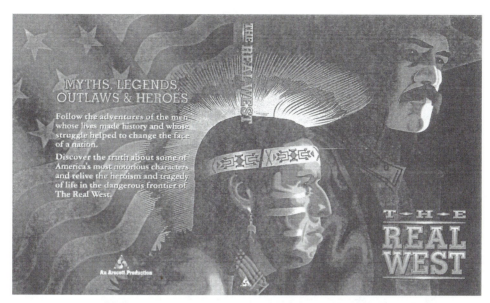

Figure 4: *The Real West*, Stephen Arscott, Grand Prize Specialty Category, CorelDRAW 5th Annual World Design Contest

Figure 5: *Potawatamie Indian*, Nick Vedros/Nick Vedros & Associates

Figure 6: *Clock Heads in Desert*, James Porto

Figure 7: *Get Real* cover,
Sunday Newsday (November 7, 1993)

Figure 8: *Puppies*, Art Rogers

Figure 9: *String of Puppies*, Jeff Koons

INDEX

original art, *See also* art
originality, 21
ownership
    copyrighting creative ideas, ix-xii
    searching for, 55-56, 59-61, 217
    See also permissions

P

PageMaker (software), 125-126
parody, 118-119, 120-121
password protection, 126-127
Past-Tints Antique Illustrations, 213, 216
payment
    copying for, 154-155
    for exclusive rights, 137-142
    for intellectual property, 156-160
pay-per-view systems, 137-138
performing rights, 25
permission letters, 57-58
permissions, 53-61
    ethics and, 156-165
    for names, 173
    obtaining online, 60
    questions about, 171-172, 173
    searching for ownership, 55-56, 59-60, 217
    when to ask for, 49
permissions specialists, 55
Perspective: The Balcony by Manet (Magritte), 7, 220
Photo Graphic Edges, 213
photomontages, 175
photos, royalty-free, 211-216
Planet Art, 213, 216
Pop Art: A Continuing History, 9
Pop Art
    brand-name images in, 9-10
    cartoon characters in, 9-10
    copying and, 7-8
    faces in, 8, 10
    tangible media and, 21-23
Portable War Memorial, The (Keinholz), 10
portable-document programs, 125-126
Porto, James, 100, 107-110, 222
Potawatamie Indian (Vedros), 100, 104-105, 221
potential markets

fair use exceptions and, 44, 46
Internet technology and, 131-132, 185
Pretty Good Privacy (PGP) (software), 129-130, 209
privacy
    computer, 133, 191
    personal, 159
property rights, 164
public domain, 31
    copyright protection and, 39-43
    evaluating works as, 54-55, 181
    summary of copyright law and, 19, 21, 98-99
    types of materials in, 177
public-key encryption, 129-130, 133
Publisher's Task Force, 213
Puppies (Rogers), 100-101, 111-115, 223
purchase orders
    buyouts in, 176-177
    signing conflicting, 144-145
    and work-for-hire provisions, 182-183

Q

QuarkXpress (software), 125-126

R

Ramos, Mel, 9
Rauschenberg, Robert, 11
read-only files, 125-126
Readymades (Duchamp), 5-6
Real West, The (Arscott), 99-100, 104-105, 221
Release 1.0. See Dyson, Esther
Rectifications (Duchamp), 6
registering copyrights, 30-31, 172, 183
Replica (software), 126
Roberts, Barbara, 108-109
Rogers, Art, 100-101, 111-115, 223
Rogers v. Koons, 100-101, 111-115, 223
Rosenquist, James, 11
royalties, 138, 157
royalty-free images, 135-136, 180, 211-216
Rushcha, Ed, 9

More from Peachpit Press

The Computer Privacy Handbook

Andre Bacard

Concerned about your privacy now that computers can track just about every area of your life? This book will make you worry even more as you read the gory details of ways computers have put our privacy in jeopardy. But you'll also learn what you can do to safeguard your electronic security. The book includes an easy-to-read manual for PGP (Pretty Good Privacy), an inexpensive e-mail encryption program. *$24.95 (300 pages)*

A Day with Biff

Ron Romain and Joe Crabtree

It's a dog-eat-dog world. Just ask Biff, a protagonist pooch who's leapt paws first into the puzzling, amusing world of humans at work. Superb usable, original clip art makes this whimsical interactive book/disk package a joy. Like any good bad dog, Biff takes his job—distracting you from the task at hand—very seriously. His weapons: a maze, a treasure hunt, and more. Now play! *$24.95 (96 pages, w/Macintosh disk)*

Designing Multimedia

Lisa Lopuck

If you're interested in being part of the booming field of multimedia, this beautifully illustrated volume shows you how. Its concept-to-product approach is highly visual: with stunning, full-color samples of actual multimedia projects. Title structure, user interface, software dynamics, and many other factors that affect design decisions are explained in detail. *$34.95 (144 pages)*

The Illustrator 6 Wow! Book

Sharon Steuer

This new edition includes eye-catching and time-saving techniques and tips for beginning through advanced users of Adobe Illustrator, using real-life "step-by-step" examples and full-page "gallery" samples from over 70 of the nation's leading Illustrator artists and designers. Covers the latest features, tools, and techniques in Illustrator 6. The accompanying CD-ROM is packed with demo versions of Illustrator 6, Photoshop 3, plug-in filters, tutorials, and many more specially created goodies. *$39.95 (224 pages w/CD-ROM)*

The Painter 4 Wow! Book

Cher Threinen-Pendarvis

Painter has so many features even power users don't know all the tricks. Whatever your skill level, you'll scurry to the computer to try out the examples in *The Painter 4 Wow! Book*. This full-color volume uses hundreds of stunning, original illustrations depicting Painter's full range of styles and effects. Step-by-step descriptions clearly explain how each piece was created by well-known artists, designers, and multimedia producers. *$44.95 (264 pages w/CD-ROM)*

The Photoshop 3 Wow! Book (Macintosh Edition)

Linnea Dayton and Jack Davis

This book is really two books in one: an easy-to-follow, step-by-step tutorial of Photoshop fundamentals, and over 150 pages of tips and techniques for getting the most out of Photoshop version 3. Full-color throughout, *The Photoshop 3 Wow! Book* shows how professional artists make the best use of Photoshop. Includes a CD-ROM containing Photoshop filters and utilities. *$39.95 (286 pages, w/CD-ROM)*

Order Form

USA 800-283-9444 • 510-548-4393 • FAX 510-548-5991
CANADA 800-387-8028 • 416-447-1779 • FAX 800-456-0536 OR 416-443-0948

Qty	Title	Price	Total
	SUBTOTAL		
	ADD APPLICABLE SALES TAX*		
	SHIPPING		
	TOTAL		

Shipping is by UPS ground: $4 for first item, $1 each add'l.

*We are required to pay sales tax in all states with the exceptions of AK, DE, HI, MT, NH, NV, OK, OR, SC and WY. Please include appropriate sales tax if you live in any state not mentioned above.

Customer Information

NAME

COMPANY

STREET ADDRESS

CITY   STATE   ZIP

PHONE (   )   FAX (   )
[REQUIRED FOR CREDIT CARD ORDERS]

Payment Method

❏ CHECK ENCLOSED   ❏ VISA   ❏ MASTERCARD   ❏ AMEX

CREDIT CARD #   EXP. DATE

COMPANY PURCHASE ORDER #

Tell Us What You Think

PLEASE TELL US WHAT YOU THOUGHT OF THIS BOOK: TITLE: _____

WHAT OTHER BOOKS WOULD YOU LIKE US TO PUBLISH?

MAC   PEACHPIT PRESS • 2414 Sixth Street • Berkeley, CA 94710